D1562655

DATE DUE

Demco, Inc. 38-294

JOHN F. KENNEDY

John F. Kennedy

by REGINA Z. KELLY

John F. Kennedy

illustrated with photographs

FOLLETT PUBLISHING COMPANY

Chicago

cover photo by
Wayne Miller, MAGNUM PHOTOS, INC.

The author gratefully acknowledges the following organizations, which permitted the reproduction of photographs on the indicated pages: United Press International, pp. 30(right), 46, 50, 91, 99, 108, 136; Wide World Photos, Inc., pp. 2, 6, 13, 20, 22, 29, 30(left), 41, 49, 54, 60, 63, 68, 72, 74, 77, 82, 85, 95, 104, 111, 114, 118, 126, 129, 134, 141, 145, 151, 155.

   ISBN 0 695-44547-2 Titan Binding
   ISBN 0 695-84547-0 Trade Binding
Library of Congress Catalog Card Number: 75-13187
Second Printing

JOHN F. KENNEDY

John Kennedy at Dexter School, Brookline, Massachusetts, 1927.

1

THE FOUR KENNEDY GIRLS and their four-year-old brother Bobby crouched on the stairs and landing of their house. Their faces were full of concern as they looked through the banisters. Downstairs, Joe and Jack were angrily slugging each other.

Rosemary shrieked. Joe had punched Jack in the nose, and blood was streaming down his face.

"Come on to the bathroom," cried Joe, and half-dragged his twelve-year-old brother by the arm.

When the two boys came out of the bathroom, Jack's face was clean, though his nose was a little red. His thick mop of red-brown hair was combed and slicked down with hair oil. He looked a little subdued, but there was no anger in the face of either boy. They fought often, but always made up quickly.

Joe looked upstairs and grinned at his sisters and Bobby. "Some of the boys from school are coming over today," he said. "Why don't you choose up sides for a game of touch football?"

Rosemary took care of Bobby, who was too young to play. The rough games of the family frightened her, even though she was the oldest girl, and she was never quick enough to take part.

In a few minutes, they were all outside, wildly chasing the football from one end of the lawn to the other with the boys from school.

The children's father, Joseph Patrick Kennedy, had moved his family to better neighborhoods as he had become more prosperous. The house in Bronxville, New York, to which they had recently moved, was a big, elegant brick house set in five acres of lawn and garden.

Joseph Kennedy by his own efforts was a millionaire. His family and their background were well known, for newspapers and magazines had told the story of his amazing rise to great wealth. He was the grandson of a poor Irish immigrant and the son of a saloon keeper.

Patrick Kennedy, the children's great-grandfather, had come to the United States from Ireland in 1849. The potato crop, almost the only means of livelihood in Ireland, had failed, and famine had followed. At least twenty million of the Irish peasantry had migrated.

Somehow, when Patrick was twenty-five, he had managed to save enough money to pay his steerage passage to Boston. All he had was the strength of his back, for he had no education. Patrick found work as a cooper, making barrels. In time, he married and had three daughters and a son, christened Patrick. Then he had died.

Young Patrick left school in his early teens and went to work on the waterfront. He was big and strong like his father, but he wanted to be more than a laborer. There were two ways in which an Irishman could make money in Boston. He could go into the liquor business, or he could enter politics. Patrick decided to do both. Somehow he managed to save until he could make a down payment on a small saloon. In time, the investment grew.

Patrick himself rarely drank anything but lemonade. When he was not at the bar, he was reading a book, usually on American history.

For the Irishman at the time, the neighborhood saloon was like a club. It was a place where he could gossip and tell his troubles. Patrick was always willing to listen and to help out those who were in need. He made many friends this way and thus gained political influence.

In 1886, Patrick Kennedy was elected to the Massachusetts House of Representatives, and six years later, to the Massachusetts Senate. He was important in the Democratic Party.

In time, Patrick married and had a son, Joseph

Patrick. Joseph attended the school connected with his family's church when he was young. But when he was fourteen, he was sent to the Boston Latin School, a private school attended by many boys from socially prominent families. "I want him to know other boys than Irish Catholics," said his father.

Patrick Kennedy chose his son's college carefully. Most of the Irish boys who went to college attended Boston College, run by Jesuit priests. "I want my boy to get something that the Jesuits can't provide," said Patrick Kennedy, and he sent Joseph to Harvard University.

That "something" in time was desired by Joseph Kennedy even more than by his father. It was the chance to become the social equal of the upper-class families of Boston. Society in Boston was different from that in most large cities in the United States. Boston society closed its doors to all but those who had been rich or important before the Civil War. No newcomer, especially if he were Irish, could break into that magic circle. The nickname of Boston was "Hub of the Universe," and the leaders of Boston really believed they were the "hub" or center of the world.

Joe Kennedy did "all right" at Harvard, according to himself. He knew he was at Harvard for much more than an education. He chose his activities and his friends carefully, giving the most attention to those that could help him the most socially. He lived at Harvard, rather than commuting by trolley as the few other Irish students did, so that he could take part in the social life there. His grades were fair. He made a letter in baseball.

He was tall and good-looking, with sandy hair and a freckled forehead. He was a graceful dancer and was liked by the Irish girls in Boston.

The Irish girl whom Joe liked the best was Rose Fitzgerald. She was the oldest and favorite daughter of John F. Fitzgerald, called "Honey Fitz," twice the Mayor of Boston and a powerful political leader. Rose was much too good for Joe Kennedy, her father thought.

The possession of wealth, power, and the chance to make a great name for himself had been Joe Kennedy's ambition since boyhood. With that in mind, he took a job as a state bank examiner after his graduation from Harvard in 1912. The job paid little, but gave him a chance to get inside information on Massachusetts banks. Because of the knowledge he gained as a bank examiner, Joe Kennedy was able to get control of the stock of a small bank that was in trouble. Accordingly, he was elected president. At the age of twenty-five, Joseph Kennedy was the youngest bank president in the state of Massachusetts.

Then Mayor Fitzgerald considered him a proper suitor for Rose. In October, 1914, Joe Kennedy and Rose Fitzgerald were married with much ceremony in the private chapel of Cardinal O'Connell of Boston. The young couple moved into a modest frame house in Brookline, a suburb of Boston. The first four children were born here: Joe, whose full name was Joseph Patrick Kennedy, Jr. in 1915; Jack, named John Fitzgerald Kennedy, after his grandfather, May 29, 1917; Rosemary, 1918; and Kathleen, 1920.

During World War I, Joe Kennedy managed a branch of a large steel corporation. He became a millionaire by 1919 when the war was over. In 1920, he moved his growing family to a large, twelve-room house in Brookline. Eunice, Patricia, and Robert were born here.

Joe Kennedy continued to make money. He became a partner in an investment firm in Boston. He began speculating in the stock market, though with many losses in the beginning. During the mid-1920's, he took over a string of movie houses in New England. Then he went to Hollywood and won control of several motion picture companies.

In the late twenties, Joe Kennedy left Hollywood and came to New York. In 1926, he moved his family

(left to right) Joseph, Jr., Rosemary, and John with Mrs. Rose Kennedy.

to New York, too, when Joe was eleven and Jack was
nine. At first, they lived in Riverdale, a suburb of New
York City. Then they moved to a house in Bronxville,
where Jean was born in 1928. Edward, the last child,
was born there in 1932.

In New York, Joseph Kennedy made more money
in the real estate business and in the liquor importing
business. He even made money at the time of the stock
market crash in October, 1929. He was strong-willed
and single-minded where business was concerned, and
he made enemies because of his methods. But nobody
could deny that Joseph Kennedy had made his money

through his own shrewd judgment and his ability to take advantage of opportunities that came his way.

In spite of the fact that Joseph Kennedy was away from his family sometimes for months at a time, his children were carefully raised and well-disciplined. This was due in part to their mother, but also because their father believed that when he was not at home, his oldest son Joseph should be in charge of the rest of the children. Although young Joe was hot-tempered and domineering, he was also generous and considerate. There were servants to help with the children, but Rose Kennedy spent much time with them herself.

The children also were watched over by their grandparents. When they lived in Boston, there was nothing Joe and Jack liked better than going out with their mother's father, "Grandpa Fitz." In Boston, he would take them to the zoo or to ride on the swan boats in the Public Garden. But best of all were the political meetings. People would cheer for Honey Fitz when he came out on the platform. If they shouted for it just a little, he would sing "Sweet Adeline," his campaign song since he had been a young man. If his rheumatism didn't bother him, he would dance an Irish jig. He held his last political office in 1922, but he kept active in everything connected with the Democratic party.

The children's Grandfather Kennedy was different. Sometimes their mother took them to visit him on Sundays. He was tall and stocky in build and had big handlebar moustaches. He was serious with the children, though always generous and kind. They sat stiffly in their chairs and hardly whispered as their mother talked to him.

One thing the Kennedy family lacked for a long time was the roots of an established home. They moved from Boston because Joe Kennedy felt his family was not accepted there. As a result, they had many homes but no real roots. The place that became home to them was the big, rambling, white frame house in Hyannis Port, Massachusetts, on Cape Cod, which Joe Kennedy bought in 1928. Later he also bought a winter home for his family at Palm Beach, Florida.

The family spent their summers and many holidays at Hyannis Port. Here Joe Kennedy taught his children to swim and sail.

Both Mr. and Mrs. Kennedy were devoted to their children and spent much time with them. When he was at home, their father took them sightseeing to places of interest. Their mother took them to every place of historical interest in Boston and nearby. They went to Bunker Hill and Paul Revere's house and the Old North Church. On longer excursions, they went to Concord and Lexington and Plymouth. At home, Jack, who loved to read, talked and read about the places they had visited.

At the dinner table, politics and current events were discussed. The children were a little in awe of their father, who seemed so well informed on every subject. He was a man with strong opinions, and he did not hesitate to express them. "Most of the talk at our dinner table were monologues by my father," Jack said later. "When we grew older, we had discussions, and my father never objected if we did not share his views."

One topic that was never discussed in the Kennedy household was money. The children had no idea about the great wealth of their father. They received only a small allowance. Once Jack wrote to his father from school and asked that his weekly allowance of forty cents be increased by thirty cents. If so, Jack argued, he would not buy "childish things" like "a chocolate marshmellow sunday." Instead he would invest his money in scout equipment "that will last for years." There is no record that the request was granted.

In order to protect his wealth and the future of his children, Joe Kennedy established trust funds for them with Mrs. Kennedy as trustee. Each child would receive a substantial income at the age of twenty-one. At the age of forty-five, each would be worth ten million dollars or more. "My father wanted us to be self-sufficient so that we could devote ourselves to public life," Jack Kennedy said later.

The children loved their father, but, perhaps, respected him more. His word was law in the household, and the children constantly tried to win his approval. The older children, Joe Kennedy insisted, were to serve as an example and take care of the younger ones. The children thus learned to depend on each other probably more than in most families.

Joe Kennedy encouraged his children to compete with each other, and to strive to excel in everything they undertook. "Second best never wins prizes," he told them. They fought each other in games and argued freely, but they were fiercely loyal and devoted to each other. All of them had warm friends, but the members of their own family were the people they liked and trusted the most. This loyalty and devotion of sisters and brothers would play an important part in Jack Kennedy's political campaigns in the future.

Whatever Joe Kennedy did was with his children in mind. To take part in politics, he believed, was the only way to leave his children a name that would be remembered. Money would be a means by which he or his children could win political recognition. His endeavor to make a fortune was largely for that goal.

2

JOE KENNEDY DIDN'T WANT HIS BOYS to go to Catholic schools. He wanted them to go to Protestant schools and meet boys who were not Catholics. When Jack was fourteen, he was sent to Choate where Joe was already enrolled. Choate was a select Episcopalian private school in Connecticut, attended by many boys from old wealthy families in New England.

Joe was a good scholar and fine athlete while at Choate. Jack, however, although he was liked by teachers and students, made only fair grades. He tried out for every team, but he was never sturdy enough to make the varsity team. Although Jack graduated only sixty-fourth in a class of 112, he was voted "most likely to succeed" by his classmates.

His teachers evidently did not share this opinion. The headmaster reported, "Casual and disorderly in almost all of his organization projects. Studies at the last minute, keeps appointments late, has little sense of material values, and can seldom locate his possessions." Keeping appointments late and not being able to locate his possessions were traits Jack Kennedy carried with him all his life.

Joseph Kennedy placed his greatest hope for winning political fame in his son Joe. He was tall, handsome, and a good athlete and scholar. Young Joe shared his father's ambition. Jack, however, had little interest in politics when he was in school.

After graduation from Choate, Jack attended Princeton briefly, but illness caused him to leave at Christmas. The following year, he enrolled at Harvard.

In the summer before Jack went to Harvard, Joe Kennedy sent him to the London School of Economics in England. Young Joe also had attended the school. Harold Laski, the noted Socialist, was a professor at the school. In his classes, Jack met people of all nationalities, many of whom were radical in their views. But Joe Kennedy wanted his sons to be informed on both sides of every issue.

Jack's first two years at Harvard were a duplicate of his career at Choate. His brother Joe won honors and played on the varsity team. Jack read a lot of history, but got poor grades in everything else. By this time, however, he and his brother Joe were good friends and got along very well.

Jack wasn't strong enough to make any of the teams, though he tried very hard. He lacked the weight, especially for football. One day in a practice game, he hit the ground hard and was slow to get up. Although he waved away helping hands, he had suffered a back injury which would trouble him for the rest of his life.

Jack Kennedy's attendance at Harvard was during the second term of President Franklin D. Roosevelt. Jack's father was an outspoken supporter of President Roosevelt, and headed important agencies in the government. In spite of this, Jack had little interest in politics. He took no part in the discussions and demonstrations at Harvard where there was strong support of Roosevelt's program.

Toward the end of 1937, Joseph Kennedy was

John Kennedy competes in the Backstroke Event at Harvard, 1938.

appointed Ambassador to Great Britain. Boston society was horrified. How could the President appoint an Irish Catholic to the highest ranking diplomatic post? But Roosevelt believed Joe Kennedy was shrewd and trustworthy and would be a keen observer.

Although Joe and Jack continued at Harvard, the other Kennedy children went to London with their parents. They lived in the thirty-six-room United States Embassy on Grosvenor Square. The young children attended the best private schools. Mrs. Kennedy, Rosemary, and Kathleen were presented at Court.

In the summer of 1937, after his second year at Harvard, Jack toured Europe with his college friend, Lem Billings. Lem was on a small budget, so they traveled in second-class coaches and stayed at cheap hotels. For the first time, Jack met people from another and interesting world. They came from many countries and classes of society. He saw the fear of dictators among the people of Europe. "People in the United States are almost completely ignorant of what is happening in Europe," he wrote to his father.

The trip was a turning point for Jack. He became interested in government, and he had an incentive now for study.

By this time, Adolf Hitler in Germany and Benito Mussolini in Italy were becoming dictators in their own countries and expanding their territory. The majority of the people in the United States at that time did not want to become involved in the wars of Europe. Congress had passed legislation designed to guarantee our neutrality.

It was not long before Ambassador Kennedy became closely associated with Neville Chamberlain, the Prime Minister of England. In spite of the growing strength of the dictators, England made no prepara-

Kennedy family in 1938: (left to right, seated) Eunice, Jean, Edward, Joseph, Sr., Patricia, Kathleen. (standing) Rosemary, Robert, John, Rose, and Joseph, Jr.

tion for war. Chamberlain and his followers believed in a policy of appeasement; that is, they hoped that if they permitted Hitler to take some of the territory which he claimed belonged to Germany, he might be satisfied. They hoped to avoid going to war for what seemed to them to be grievances of other countries. With all of this, Ambassador Kennedy agreed. He was a strong isolationist; that is, he did not want the United States to become involved in the wars of Europe.

In his third year at Harvard, Jack was permitted to spend a semester in Europe. This was a critical time. Hitler had invaded a part of Czechoslovakia. Following this, Chamberlain and Edouard Deladier, the Premier of France, met with Hitler and Mussolini in Munich, Germany. Hitler promised that he would seek no more territory. In the middle of March, 1939, however, Hitler broke his promise and conquered the rest of Czechoslovakia. The British now realized that this was the end of appeasement. On March 31, Britain guaranteed the independence of Poland. This meant that Britain would fight if Poland were invaded.

During the spring and summer of 1939, Jack traveled through Europe, Russia, the Balkans, and Palestine. He was a guest at the various Embassies of the United States. From each country he sent his father a report of all that he saw and heard. From Germany he wrote, "The German people are being whipped into a fierce hatred of the British." When he was in Poland, he wrote his father, "The Polish people will never give up Danzig without fighting." Danzig was Poland's only outlet to the sea.

On August 23, while Jack was in Berlin, Germany and Russia signed a treaty not to fight each other. When Jack returned to London a few days later, he brought his father a message from the United States Embassy in Berlin. "War will break out in Europe within one week," it stated.

At dawn on September 1, the Germans invaded Poland. Two days later, early in the morning, Chamberlain sent for Joseph Kennedy and read to him the British declaration of war against Germany. It would be announced on radio that morning.

"It's the end of the world, the end of everything," said Ambassador Kennedy when he telephoned the news to President Roosevelt.

There were busy hours now for the United States Ambassador to Great Britain. Mrs. Kennedy and the children were sent to a house in the country until they could safely leave England. Joe and Jack stayed to help their father. Preparations were made to send home the nine thousand Americans living in England.

At three A.M. on September 4, the Germans torpedoed a British liner with 300 Americans aboard. As soon as Ambassador Kennedy heard the news, he hurried to Jack's bedroom. He sent Jack to Glasgow, Scotland, where the survivors were being brought. Jack made arrangements to send the Americans to the United States and telephoned information to his father. Jack handled the assignment well. It was the first time he had been given such a large responsibility.

By the end of September, the Germans were in control of all of Poland. After that, all war activity ceased, and Chamberlain predicted that soon there would be peace. However, Mrs. Kennedy and the family returned to the United States. Joe and Jack went with them. Joe was to attend the Yale Law School, and Jack was to finish his final year at Harvard.

"I am considered quite a seer here," Jack wrote to his father. This was probably true. Perhaps no other student at Harvard had had the rare opportunity to be as close to the outbreak of war in Europe as Jack Kennedy.

In his senior year at Harvard, John Kennedy worked hard to make up for the credits he had lost while he was in Europe. He wanted to graduate with honors, especially in the writing of his thesis for graduation.

With the memory of what he had observed in

Europe and his knowledge of the situation in England, Kennedy decided to write on *Appeasement at Munich*. He spent many hours in the library, and had been given information by the American Embassies in Europe and by his father which he could not have obtained anywhere else.

John Kennedy got a grade of *magna cum laude* (with great praise) for his thesis, and graduated with honors. Some of the professors suggested to Kennedy that he rewrite his thesis and try to have it published. With the help of Arthur Krock, a newspaper columnist who was an admirer and an old friend of the Ambassador, Kennedy rewrote and improved his essay. He changed the title to *Why England Slept*. Henry R. Luce, the publisher of *Time, Life*, and *Fortune* magazines, and also a friend of the Ambassador, wrote the foreword. The book was published in July, 1940, and got good reviews. Jack Kennedy donated his British royalties to the bombed town of Plymouth, England.

April 22

3

IN THE MEANTIME, the war in Europe had been renewed. Soon the Germans were marching victoriously through Denmark, Norway, Belgium, Holland, and finally France. England was bombed from the air and its fleet almost destroyed.

Although the Kennedy family was safe in the United States, Ambassador Kennedy had been in 244 air raids in London. Once his automobile was thrown on the sidewalk by an exploding bomb, but he escaped unharmed.

In the United States, we began to move toward preparation for war. John Kennedy was uncertain about his future after his graduation from Harvard. Should he become a writer? Should he study law like Joe? Should he go into politics or business? How would the war affect his plans?

Joe volunteered and was accepted for Navy aviation training. Shortly after his twenty-fourth birthday, Jack tried to enlist in the Army but was rejected because of his back injury. Then he tried to enlist in the Navy, and was rejected for the same reason.

For the next few months, he exercised to strengthen his back. Finally, in September, 1941, he passed the Navy fitness test. At first, he was assigned to do desk work in the Navy Intelligence office. Then on December 7, 1941, Pearl Harbor, our great Naval base in the Hawaiian Islands, was bombed in a surprise attack by the Japanese. The following day, the United States declared war on Japan. Kennedy was anxious now to get into the action. Finally he asked his father to use his influence to get him assigned to sea duty. Late in 1942, he was assigned to the Motor Boat Torpedo Squadron.

For six months, Kennedy trained in the handling of PT boats. The job of the PT boats was to intercept the enemy destroyers. Their base was at Rendova Harbor on Lumberi Island in the Pacific. By March, 1943, he was a lieutenant junior grade in charge of PT boat 109.

On August 2, 1943, Lieutenant Kennedy's boat was patroling Blackett Strait in the mid-Solomons. PT 109 was part of a big, well-planned attack on the Japanese in the area. The night was black. Kennedy was at the wheel, staring out into the darkness. Only one motor of his boat was running, to keep down the noise. Suddenly, about two-thirty in the morning, a Japanese destroyer bore down on PT 109.

"All men to your stations!" shouted Kennedy, as

Lieut. (j.g.) Kennedy (standing, extreme right) and crew of PT 109.

he did his best to turn his boat to starboard. Then, "Fire all guns! Fire all torpedoes!"

The crew watched in horror. There was nothing they could do. In a few minutes, the destroyer went through the PT boat with a horrible crunching sound, and cut it in two as cleanly as if it had been done with a sharp knife. The gasoline tanks ignited in seconds. One portion of the boat caught on fire and exploded. The bow was still afloat. The sea was on fire all around.

Kennedy was thrown on his back on the part that remained up. There were cries for help now as those who had been thrown overboard struggled to swim away from the gasoline burning on the water. Kennedy and the other men who had been thrown with him onto the boat swam to help the survivors in the water. Two men had been lost. One had been badly burned, and another had severe leg injuries. Kennedy was in the water for three hours as he swam and tugged the survivors to what was left of their boat.

"What do you want to do? Fight or surrender?" Kennedy asked his men when all were on board. They knew that there were Japanese in all the islands around them. The half of the PT boat was slowly sinking now. They finally decided to attempt to swim to the next island three miles away, which might be free of Japanese.

"I'll take care of McMahon," said Kennedy. McMahon was the sailor who had been badly hurt. Kennedy attached a long strap to McMahon's life jacket. Then, with the strap in his teeth, he swam and tugged the injured man. Those who could not swim propelled a plank like a raft and clung to it. It took five hours to reach the island.

That night, Jack Kennedy swam to a place the PT boats passed when they planned an attack. Although he swam and trod water nearly all night, he saw no boats. In the morning, he returned to the island exhausted from his ordeal. He had worn little besides shoes, and his body was cut from the sharp edges of the coral on the reefs against which he had been thrown by high waves.

The next night, George Ross swam to the same

place with no better luck than Kennedy had had.

All the men were hungry and thirsty now, for they had had no food or water since their attack. On the third day, they decided to swim to the next island. The difficult swim was worth life itself, because there were a few coconuts on the second island, and the men were able to quench their thirst.

On the fourth day, Kennedy and Ross swam to Nauru Island, which was next in position. The island had been abandoned by the Japanese, and the two men found food and water and a canoe. They returned with these to the other men, and then Kennedy went back in the canoe to Nauru Island.

"Rendova! Rendova!" he said to some friendly natives. They seemed to understand. On the smooth side of a coconut, the young lieutenant carved a message: "ELEVEN ALIVE NATIVE KNOWS POSIT AND REEFS NAURU ISLAND KENNEDY."

That night, Kennedy and Ross went out in the canoe to look for PT boats, for they were not sure that the message on the coconut would be delivered. A storm arose. Their canoe was overturned, and they were thrown on a reef. Somehow they struggled to the beach on Nauru Island and then fell asleep.

The next morning, someone shook Jack Kennedy awake. Four natives had come to the island with a letter from the commander of the New Zealand infantry. Kennedy and Ross returned to the other men and told them of the news. Then Kennedy was put in a canoe and covered with palm leaves, so that he would not be detected by Japanese flying overhead, and taken to the base. Soon a PT boat guided by the natives rescued the other men.

In the United States, the crew had already been listed as lost, and a memorial service had been held. Joe Kennedy had received the customary telegram from the Navy Department that is sent to a sailor's family to report him missing, but had not as yet told the family. Their first news was an announcement over the radio that Lieutenant John F. Kennedy and his crew had been saved.

"Saved from what?" Mrs. Kennedy asked her husband. Then he told her what had happened.

To his son, Joe Kennedy sent a message in whose sentiments all the family shared: "Thank God for your deliverance."

For the first time, Jack Kennedy had acted on his own initiative and, through his courage and enterprise, had solved a difficult situation. It was a turning point in his life.

Kennedy was awarded the Purple Heart and also the Navy and Marine Corps Medal. However, active service was ended for him. His back injury had been greatly aggravated by the swimming and tugging he had done. He contracted malaria, and his weight went down to 125 pounds. He returned to the United States and entered the Chelsea Naval Hospital near Boston to recuperate. He retired from the Navy at the end of 1945.

On August 2, 1944, the whole Kennedy family, except for Joe, were at their home in Hyannis Port to celebrate the anniversary of the attack on Jack's PT boat. Jack was home for the weekend. In the afternoon, two Catholic chaplains from the Navy came to the house and asked to speak to Mr. Kennedy. The priests had a sad message. Young Joe had been killed in action. He had been in active service and had been

(left photo) Captain F. L. Conklin pins medal on John F. Kennedy.
(right photo) Lieutenant (j.g.) Joseph Kennedy, Jr., as aerial patrolman.

given orders to return home. However, before leaving England, he and another pilot had volunteered for a dangerous mission. They were to fly a load of explosives to a Nazi submarine base. Their plane had blown apart just before they were ready to parachute out, and both men had been killed.

Somehow Joe Kennedy managed to return to the family and tell them what had happened. It was the first great tragedy in the family. Kathleen was killed in a plane crash in Europe in 1948. Others were to come. But for a time, it seemed to Joe Kennedy as if the end of all hope in the future had come to him. All of his ambition to win political honor for his family had been centered in his oldest son. Young Joe was handsome, bright, likable, and ambitious. In his boyhood he had openly stated that he intended to become President of the United States, and his father had never denied that this might not be possible. Now all that he had striven for to bring this about seemed to have come to an end. It was years before Joe Kennedy could even speak to anyone outside his family about his oldest son.

There was a tradition in the Kennedy family. Each boy had his place, and had to earn the right to move up to the next level. Young Ted got the sailboats ready for his older brothers. Bobby had done it before him. Joe and Jack had made ready their father's sailboat.

In public service it was the same. Nineteen-year-old Bobby enlisted in the Navy after Joe died to take Joe's place in the war effort. Jack must now be the son to work for a political career.

John Kennedy's start in politics came in 1945 guided largely by his father. There was an opening for a new representative in Congress from the Eleventh Congressional District in Massachusetts. The Eleventh District covered a wide area. It included some of the worst slums in the country, as well as wealthy neighborhoods like Cambridge where Harvard University was. The seat was highly desired, and there were ten candidates including Kennedy who wanted the Democratic nomination.

Of all the candidates, Kennedy was the least known. He was almost a stranger in Boston. The Kennedys had not lived there since Jack was nine years old. He rented a small apartment to establish a residence. It remained his only Boston home. When he later built a house, it was at Hyannis Port. His political headquarters were at the Bellevue Hotel in Boston. Honey Fitz lived there, and so did many old-line politicians.

Jack Kennedy did not seem to have any of the qualities of a politician. He was shy and withdrawn. He did not mix well with new people. It was hard for him to flatter. He was nervous and hesitant when he made speeches. His opponents scornfully referred to him as a "poor little rich boy."

Kennedy seemed so young, too, though he was twenty-eight years old. He was still very thin after his ordeal in the Pacific. His mop of hair and unlined face gave him a boyish look. His Harvard accent and background of wealth, travel, and good schooling made him seem far apart from the dreary, poverty-stricken people to whom he talked.

But there was something that must have won their hearts as he held out his hand, gave a wide, flashing smile, and asked them to vote for him. In a few minutes there would be smiles and friendly words in reply, as with sincere interest he talked to them about their problems. Once his father watched in astonishment as Jack moved among a group of Italian workmen. "I never thought he had it in him," said Joe Kennedy.

But Jack Kennedy had assets that other candidates did not possess. The name of Kennedy was magic. His grandfathers on both sides had been political leaders in Boston. The newspapers and magazines for years had reported Joe Kennedy's rise to fortune.

Unlimited money would be spent on advertising, radio appearances, public opinion polls, and so on. The whole Kennedy family rallied to his support. Chums from college and Navy buddies also helped. They were young and fresh and a different breed from the politicians of the past. "The New Generation offers a leader," was their slogan.

The Kennedy girls rang doorbells, talked in a friendly manner, and handed out leaflets about their brother. Bob Kennedy rang doorbells, ate countless plates of spaghetti in Italian neighborhoods, and played softball with the kids. So did Jack and all the young people who helped him. There were a half dozen house parties each night, and somehow, the candidate managed to get to all of them. Joe Kennedy did no street canvassing. He used the telephone to talk to people of influence.

Mrs. Kennedy had learned how to campaign as a girl when she worked to elect her father, Mayor John Fitzgerald. She wore her mink coat and jewels in Cambridge. After a brief talk about her son, she would tell the women about the latest fashions in Paris. In the poor neighborhoods, she dressed simply. There she talked about how she ran her big household and kept a card index on her nine children about their diseases and school problems.

The climax of the campaign was a big party given by the Kennedys at a Boston hotel. Hand-addressed engraved invitations had been sent out for a reception in honor of the candidate and his family. There were fifteen hundred women who came in their best gowns and went down the receiving line and then to the well-filled tables. At the head of the receiving line, in white tie and tails, was the former Ambassador to Great Britain, Joseph P. Kennedy. It was the last time he would appear in public for his son. "Everybody wants to be in society with the Kennedys," was the bitter comment of one of Kennedy's opponents.

At first, Jack Kennedy had felt uneasy about running for office. "I'm just filling Joe's shoes," he frequently said to those who worked with him. "If he were alive, I'd never be in this." But as the campaign went on, the Kennedy drive and spirit began to show in him. Now he wanted to win, not because of his father's ambition, but because he himself wanted to come out on top.

Kennedy won a tremendous victory in the primary. He received forty percent of all the votes cast, and had twice as many votes as his nearest competitor. At the headquarters that night, Honey Fitz stood on a table and managed to dance an Irish jig while he sang "Sweet Adeline." In the election in November, Kennedy beat his Republican opponent by a two-to-one margin.

But it had taken more than money, the help of

the family, and a background of political leadership to win the election for Jack Kennedy. Other sons of fathers who are wealthy or prominent in politics have tried for office and have lost. There were other factors that made Kennedy win this election and all those in which he ran. He had begun his campaign early. He had worked long and tirelessly each day. When he spoke, it was on the issues that concerned the people who would vote for him. When they listened, his sincerity and personal charm came through and they believed in him.

The success of Jack Kennedy's first campaign was repeated in 1948 and 1950. He was reelected to the House of Representatives both times without even trying very hard. He was given good committee assignments, and in time, it was thought, he might become Speaker of the House.

He had no definite principles or convictions as yet. He continued to share his father's views, though he began to differ on foreign policy. What was best for the people of Massachusetts influenced John Kennedy's viewpoint most of all. He, therefore, fought for low-cost housing and other social welfare programs.

By 1952, Kennedy's seat in the House was assured, but he was not satisfied to remain. "We were just worms in the House," he said later. "Nobody paid attention to us nationally."

A Senate seat was open in Massachusetts in 1952. Long before that date, he had begun to campaign. He accepted every invitation to speak or be a guest at some ceremony. By the time he announced he was a candidate in April, 1952, his name was well-known all over Massachusetts.

Henry Cabot Lodge was Kennedy's Republican opponent. Most people thought that Lodge would be a hard man to beat. He was well liked and had a good record. Like Jack Kennedy, he had wealth and a political background. His grandfather, Senator Henry Cabot Lodge, had been a leading senator at the time of President Woodrow Wilson. In addition, Lodge had something for which Joseph Kennedy had long aimed: social position. Lodge was a member of an old and highly-placed family in Massachusetts.

Once again, the Kennedy family campaigned for the oldest son, in much the same manner as in Jack's first campaign. Again the house parties and receptions were given and attended by the Kennedys. "Coffee with the Kennedys" became a standard social pattern in the campaign. The fact that all the family worked together troubled the supporters of Lodge. "I don't worry about the Kennedy money," said one. "It's that family of his. They're all over the state."

Robert Kennedy was Jack's campaign manager now, although he was not quite twenty-seven years old and had had no experience as a manager. He astonished the professionals by his efficient and thorough methods.

"The campaign was the most thoroughly detailed and smoothly run campaign in the history of Massachusetts, and possibly anywhere else," wrote one political observer.

Much of the time throughout the campaign, Jack Kennedy was in great pain, due to his back injury. Often he had to move on crutches, though not in public. "When he came to the door of a hall," said a friend, "he

Congressman John Kennedy with his campaign workers on the night of his election to the Senate, 1952.

would hand the crutches to someone, and march down the aisle as straight as a West Point cadet. How he did it, I'll never know."

On election night, the Kennedy supporters watched the returns with concern in the early part of the evening. This was the year in which Dwight D. Eisenhower ran as a Republican against Democratic Governor Adlai Stevenson of Illinois for President. As the vote of Eisenhower piled up all over the nation, it also went up in Massachusetts. Would Senator Lodge be swept in with the Republican tide? Only Jack Kennedy seemed unconcerned and sure of victory. He went to a movie in the early evening.

At six o'clock the next morning, Lodge conceded his defeat. Kennedy had won by 70,000 votes, although both Stevenson and Democrat Paul J. Dever, who had run for Governor of Massachusetts, had been defeated. Honey Fitz was dead by now, but one old Irishman said he was sure the old man must be singing "Sweet Adeline" and dancing an Irish jig in heaven.

4

KENNEDY LIKED THE DIGNITY of the Senate and the history associated with it. The door of his office in the Senate building was always open to those who wanted help. He had a large staff, for he did not have to spare expense, and he also had an office and staff in Boston. Each year, he donated his Senate salary to charity.

Kennedy's youthful appearance contrasted with that of most of his colleagues. There are stories told of how he was mistaken for a Senate page, and called "laddie" by another senator. But in his work and speeches, he soon proved that he had the maturity of his years. He was thirty-five when he was elected.

Life was pleasant and comfortable for him in Washington. He leased a house in the Georgetown area of the city. Kennedy was young, good-looking, very popular in society, and had a pleasant personality and a quick wit. He became Washington's "gay young bachelor." But Senator Kennedy, though he liked girls, did not think of getting married, for the time, at least.

In January, 1953, Senator Kennedy secured the services of a twenty-four-year-old lawyer, Theodore

Sorenson, as one of his legislative assistants. Sorenson was from Nebraska. His father was a Progressive Republican who had supported the programs of Franklin Delano Roosevelt. Like the Kennedys, the Sorensons were always deeply interested in politics and government service.

Ted Sorenson had none of the background of great wealth or high society in which Senator Kennedy had always moved. But the two men were alike in temperament, intelligence, and beliefs.

At first Sorenson was given the job of working on New England affairs, though up to that time, he had never been to New England. His thorough grasp of the problems made Kennedy soon appoint him as his first assistant. Later on, Sorenson became Kennedy's chief speech writer. So similar were their ideas and methods of expression that it was hard to tell who worked the most on the speeches. The two men became devoted to each other and worked almost as a unit. Except for his brother Robert, no one was closer to Kennedy than Ted Sorenson.

Senator Kennedy did not want to be labeled either as a liberal or conservative Democrat. He believed in following a middle-of-the-road policy. When he had been in the House in 1948, he had won the enmity of the conservative American Legion at a time when they were opposing a veterans' housing bill which he supported. In a speech, he stated that the leadership of the American Legion hadn't had a "constructive thought since 1918."

Later when Kennedy was a Senator, he got into trouble with the extreme liberals in his party by stating in an interview that he had never joined certain extremely liberal organizations. "I'm not comfortable with those people," he said. There was quite an uproar by the liberals after the statement was made. The members of one organization said that they weren't quite comfortable with Senator Kennedy.

Kennedy's chief interest when he was a Senator as when he was in the House was in the passage of laws that would help New England. However, he did not always win approval from his supporters in New England. Sometimes he voted for projects that would serve the whole nation in spite of opposition from his section.

Jack Kennedy was considered the "most eligible bachelor in Washington." At a dinner party in 1951, Kennedy met Jacqueline Bouvier. He had met her briefly before. But this time, as he said later, he "leaned across the asparagus" and asked her for a date.

Jacqueline was twenty-one at the time, and Kennedy was twelve years older. She had beautiful features, dark hair and eyes, and a soft, lovely voice. Her background was something like that of Kennedy, though her family had moved in high society for generations. She was a Roman Catholic, had grown up in New York, and had attended private girls' schools. She had gone to Vassar for two years and after that to France to study at the Sorbonne. In Paris she had lived with a French family and learned to speak French fluently. She also spoke Spanish and Italian.

Senator Kennedy and Jacqueline were married on September 12, 1953, in St. Mary's Roman Catholic Church in Newport, Rhode Island, where her family had a large summer home and an estate. Reverend

John Kennedy and Jacqueline Bouvier, Hyannis Port, Mass., 1953.

Richard J. Cushing, then the Archbishop of Boston, performed the ceremony, and the Pope sent a papal blessing. The wedding was the social event of the summer.

Marriage did not change Kennedy very much. He was still absent-minded and mislaid articles. He hated to waste a minute. He would read while he was shaving or relaxing in a tub. He was able to flick through a magazine or newspaper while he was talking to someone, but be fully aware of what had been said. He would be indignant if he got to an appointment ahead of time.

"He has incredible energy and is always in a hurry, even during our quiet evenings at home," said his wife. He was called "Young Man in a Hurry" in a magazine article about him, and the title was a good description.

The Kennedys lived and entertained simply in their house in the Georgetown section of Washington. Best of all, they enjoyed having a few close friends for dinner and an evening of lively conversation. Jackie liked music, the theater, the ballet, and the works and society of writers and artists. She herself was a good amateur painter and cartoonist.

Her husband had little interest in the arts and liked a good movie more than any other form of entertainment. Jackie, in turn, knew and understood little about politics. But through association with Jackie her husband learned more about the arts, and in time she learned more about politics. In order to keep up with the political talk in the evenings in her home, she took courses in political science and history at Georgetown University.

Kennedy's spinal trouble grew worse after his marriage until he was forced to use crutches all the time. An operation was possible but risky. "I'd rather die than spend my life using these things," he said, kicking his crutches.

The operation was performed in October, 1954, in New York. Twice his wife and family were called to his bedside when it seemed that he would die. In December, he went by plane to his father's home at Palm Beach, but he showed little improvement.

In the middle of February, he had another operation. Once more he received the last rites of the Catholic Church, for death seemed near. However, he recovered and again went to Florida to convalesce. He realized that although he would suffer pain, his back would not cripple him.

During the months of convalescence in Florida, Kennedy worked on the book he later called *Profiles in Courage*. It was a collection of true stories about political leaders and the crises they had faced in order to

Senator and Mrs. Kennedy leaving New York hospital for Florida.

defend the unpopular causes for which they stood. Nearly all of the leaders had lost political power because of the stand they took. Ted Sorenson helped with the research and writing. The book was published in 1956, and the following year won the Pulitzer Prize for biography.

Kennedy returned to the Senate toward the end of May, after an absence of nine months. There was a celebration to welcome him, and his offices were filled with newspapermen and photographers.

In 1956, it was expected that Governor Stevenson

again would be the candidate of the Democratic party for President. Stevenson, however, let it be known that he probably would let the convention choose the candidate for Vice-President. Months before the convention, Kennedy decided that he would work for this office. Being on the ticket with Stevenson would give him national importance. His father was against the idea, for he was sure Eisenhower would be reelected. "I was afraid Jack would be blamed for the defeat because he was a Catholic," said the Ambassador later. "That would make it much more difficult for another Catholic to run in the future."

Kennedy's other advisers, however, thought that

Senator John Kennedy placing the name of Adlai Stevenson in nomination for the Presidency, Chicago, 1956.

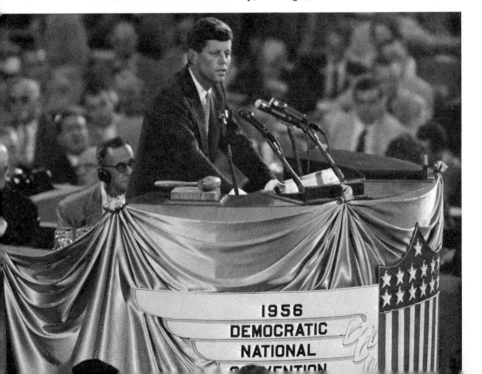

having a Catholic on the ticket would strengthen the chances of a victory for the Democratic party. Stevenson himself liked and approved of Kennedy. Some of the older Democratic leaders were against Kennedy. They thought him too young and without experience.

The Democratic convention was in August in Chicago at the International Amphitheater. Stevenson had asked Kennedy to make the nominating speech, and on the first ballot, Stevenson was named the Democratic candidate for President.

Then Stevenson announced, "I have concluded to depart from the precedents of the past so that the selection of the Vice-President may be made by the convention."

There was little time to organize a campaign for the votes of the delegates before the next session of the convention. But the Kennedy team went into action with its usual vigor. From a hotel room nearby, Kennedy and his aides watched the convention on television. Senator Estes Kefauver of Tennessee, who had won national fame for his frequently televised appearances as he investigated the crime syndicate, was Kennedy's chief opponent.

On the first ballot, Kefauver was in the lead, but Kennedy was a close second. On the second ballot,

Kennedy's vote moved closer to that of Kefauver. The third ballot started. Some of the states began switching their votes to Kefauver. In a short time, Kefauver had the majority.

"That's it. Let's go," said Kennedy. He was bitterly disappointed, but as always, he was outwardly calm and controlled.

In a few minutes, he was pushing his way through the crowd in the convention hall and was on the platform. "Ladies and gentlemen," he cried, and he managed to smile. "I want to express my appreciation to Democrats from all parts of the country who have been so kind to me this afternoon." Then he moved that Senator Kefauver be named by acclamation, which was done.

Because of his personal popularity, President Eisenhower was elected for a second term. However, the Democrats won control in both the House and the Senate. Lyndon B. Johnson became the Majority Leader in the Senate.

Kefauver had won the nomination for the Vice-Presidency, but the real hero of the contest was John F. Kennedy. The whole nation had seen a fine-looking young man accept his defeat with a smile. His campaign for the Presidency probably began at that moment.

5

"SENATOR KENNEDY IS ON THE MAKE," wrote James Reston, the chief Washington correspondent for the influential newspaper, the *New York Times*. "He makes no pretense about it. He dismisses suggestions that he is too young for the Presidency."

Beginning with October, 1956, Kennedy made many speeches, wrote articles for magazines, and traveled to all parts of the country to preside at special events. In addition, the magazines were filled with articles about the "amazing Kennedy family," and about the Senator himself and his wife. "The surest way to sell a magazine," it was said, "is to have a picture of one of the Kennedys on the cover." There was increased interest in the young Senator and his beautiful wife when they had a baby, Caroline, in November, 1957.

In 1958, Kennedy was reelected to the Senate by the highest vote ever won by a senator in Massachusetts. The Republicans had run a comparatively unknown candidate against him, for they were sure that Kennedy would win. He used the same methods of campaigning as in the past. However, besides touring

Massachusetts, he traveled to other states and spoke in behalf of other Democrats who were running for office. More and more, John F. Kennedy was becoming known all over the United States.

Late in October, 1959, Kennedy met with his closest advisers in the living room of his brother Robert's home in Hyannis Port. They were meeting to make their plans for the nomination of Senator Kennedy as the Democratic candidate for the Presidency. Sorenson was to be the chief speech writer. Bob Kennedy again was to manage the campaign. On January 2, 1960, Kennedy announced that he was a candidate for the presidential nomination.

Theodore Sorenson

There were many obstacles to Kennedy's nomination. Few men have been elected President if their only prominence has been in the House or Senate. Many of our Presidents have been popular military heroes or governors. A governor is on record largely with the issues of his own state. A senator votes on national issues. "No matter how you vote," said Kennedy, "somebody is made unhappy."

However, Kennedy's youth and religion were his biggest handicaps. In 1960, he would be forty-three years old, a mature age, though young for a President. But he looked much younger. The fact that he was a Roman Catholic was an even greater obstacle. Only one Roman Catholic, Governor Alfred E. Smith of New York, had ever run for the Presidency, and he had been badly defeated. "If I were governor of a large state, fifty-five years old, and a Protestant, I could sit back and let the nomination come to me," said Kennedy. "But if I'm going to get it, I'll have to work for it."

Prominent political leaders who were Catholics, like Mayor Wagner of New York, Governor Brown of California, and Governor Lawrence of Pennsylvania, were against Kennedy's nomination. They thought he would be defeated if nominated. That would hold back the chance of any other Catholic being nominated in the future, just as the defeat of Governor Smith was now affecting the way politicians thought about John F. Kennedy.

There was nothing in Kennedy's record as a Senator that would indicate he would favor the Catholics. He had voted against sending an ambassador to the Vatican. Free bus transportation and health services were all that he had asked be given to the Catholic schools. He insisted that no Catholic had ever asked him for anything that was not in the public interest.

However, there was unreasoning fear among many Protestants of the power of the Pope over members of the Catholic Church. The Pope is the ruler of a country, the Vatican State, as well as the head of the Catholic Church, they remembered. He has the power to "excommunicate," that is, to drive a Catholic out of the Church. Therefore the Pope could force Catholics to obey the rulings of the Church.

Gloomily at times Kennedy thought that the sign "Only Protestants need apply," which used to be on the doors of factories in Massachusetts, should also be hanging on the door of the White House.

Another issue that gave Kennedy great trouble, especially among liberals, was the record of his attitude toward Senator Joseph McCarthy of Wisconsin. Senator McCarthy had been head of the committee in

Congress which had investigated the activities of Communists in our government in the 1950's. McCarthy had been ruthless in his methods and often unfair.

Resentment against McCarthy's purpose as well as his methods had grown in Congress and among the people. Many Congressmen, however, were afraid to come out openly against him. They had seen instances where someone who had opposed him had been defeated in an election.

Although Kennedy had not approved of McCarthy's methods, there were personal reasons why he had not come out strongly against him. His brother Robert, who had become a lawyer, had worked for a time on McCarthy's committee. Later Robert Kennedy had resigned because he did not agree with the views of the committee. McCarthy also was a good friend of Ambassador Kennedy and had been a guest in the house in Hyannis Port. In addition, many people in Massachusetts supported McCarthy mainly because he was a Catholic. In his campaign in 1952, Kennedy had managed to evade making any statement about McCarthy.

In July, 1954, a resolution had been proposed in the Senate to censure McCarthy for "conduct unbecoming a Senator." The measure was postponed, and so Kennedy had not voted. In October, he had entered the hospital for his operation. When the motion to censure McCarthy came up again in December, Kennedy was in the hospital and again did not vote. The resolution had been passed by a large majority. Many liberals, especially Mrs. Franklin D. Roosevelt, who was influential in the Democratic party, never forgave Kennedy for not taking a stand, even though his illness gave him an excuse.

There were strong leaders in the Democratic party who, in the beginning, seemed to have a much better chance than Kennedy to win the nomination. Chief among these was Senator Lyndon B. Johnson of Texas, the Majority Leader in the Senate.

Another leading candidate was Senator William Stuart Symington of Missouri. In President Truman's administration, Symington had been appointed to several important posts, and had become Secretary of the Air Force.

Senator Hubert Horatio Humphrey of Minnesota was also a leading candidate. He had been Mayor of Minneapolis from 1945 to 1947 and was important in Minnesota politics. He was a strong liberal.

The unknown quantity for nomination was Governor Adlai Stevenson of Illinois. Although Stevenson had been twice defeated for the Presidency, he still had a large and devoted following who were determined to have him nominated for a third time. Stevenson himself had announced that he would not be a candidate because he had been twice defeated. "Deep down," said a friend, "he wants the nomination. But he wants the convention to come to him." Although Stevenson made no move to win delegates, neither did he endorse any of the other candidates for office.

The political bosses of the Democratic party thought that either Johnson or Symington would be the candidate most likely to appeal to the voters. Humphrey, they thought, was too liberal. Kennedy was a Catholic and too young for the office. Stevenson was a two-time loser and also a liberal. The only way that Kennedy and Humphrey could show the bosses that the people wanted either one was to enter the primary elections in the states.

A primary election in a state is one in which the members of a party vote for the person they want to be nominated. The outcome is not binding on the delegates to the nominating conventions, but the primaries are important in showing how the voters are thinking. Sixteen states held primary elections. Entering a primary is a hard and expensive task. Often both the candidate and his funds are exhausted before the real race begins. Kennedy entered seven of the primaries, and Humphrey entered five.

The first real contest between the two men was in

John Kennedy salutes Hubert Humphrey on the night of Kennedy's victory in the 1960 Wisconsin Democratic primary election.

Wisconsin. Here Humphrey seemed to have the advantage. Wisconsin was a farm state and near his home state of Minnesota, and two-thirds of the people were Protestants.

Kennedy campaigned as usual. Bareheaded and without a topcoat, he would be out early in the morning to greet the workers. "My name is Kennedy. I'm running for President in the primary," he would say with a pleasant grin and handshake. Again and again he gave his reasons for wanting to be President. "It is the key office in American life. The President alone can shape, create, and protect the country."

Both men spent about the same amount of money in Wisconsin. But Kennedy had a large number of unpaid volunteers working for him, and the convenience and comfort of traveling in his own plane. The Kennedy family had bought a large jet plane, and it was rented to Kennedy's organization for the campaign. "It was like an independent grocer competing against a chain store," said Humphrey.

Kennedy won six out of the ten districts in Wisconsin, but his victory was not decisive. Nor could Lou Harris, his principal poll taker, tell whether religion had been an issue in the election. Kennedy decided he would try in West Virginia where only five percent of the people were Catholics.

On the other hand, Humphrey was encouraged by the results in Wisconsin because he had expected a bad defeat. He also decided to run in West Virginia. He was not aware that the party bosses had already decided that he had no chance. Their opinion was that if he could not win in Wisconsin where everything seemed to be in his favor, he could not win in the whole country.

West Virginia had been a solidly Democratic state since the time of Franklin Delano Roosevelt. Coal mining was the big industry, but each year the industry had declined as more and more oil and gas were used for fuel. In one county, a fourth of the people were on relief.

Again, Humphrey seemed to have the advantage.

Not only was he a Protestant, but as a liberal, he had far more appeal than Kennedy. But West Virginia was a state with many war heroes and a record of war volunteers. The story of Kennedy's heroism in World War II stirred the imagination of the people.

The sincerity of his speeches and appearance when he was on television appealed to them. The openness with which he expressed his views on religion convinced them. "Is anyone going to tell me that I lost this primary forty-two years ago on the day I was baptized?" he asked the crowds.

As always, the Kennedy volunteers and efficient organization swept over the state. Another big asset for Kennedy was that Franklin Delano Roosevelt, Jr., the son of the former President, campaigned for Kennedy in West Virginia. Young Roosevelt looked and talked like his father, and the people of West Virginia had not forgotten that the relief measures passed in the time of President Roosevelt had saved the poverty-stricken people of the state.

Long before midnight on election day, Kennedy was in the lead by a two-to-one margin. It was a complete and stunning victory. Late that night, Humphrey announced he was no longer a candidate. Kennedy thought he had buried the religious issue once and for all.

Following the victory in West Virginia, Kennedy's chances for nomination were like a snowball going downhill, as he piled up one primary success after another. By the time of the Democratic convention, he had committed to him about 600 of the 761 votes needed to win the nomination.

The Democratic convention was in Los Angeles in mid-July in the Sports Arena. Governor Stevenson still denied that he was seeking the nomination, but there was growing enthusiasm for him, especially in Los Angeles where he had many followers. Each day pickets paraded around the Sports Arena carrying signs for Stevenson. Chief among those who favored

John (left), Robert (center), and Edward Kennedy, Hyannis Port, 1960.

Stevenson was Mrs. Franklin D. Roosevelt. The first big demonstration at the convention was when Stevenson entered the hall to take his seat as a delegate when the convention opened.

With the same thoroughness and expertness with which he had managed the previous campaigns, Bob Kennedy tallied the votes for his brother before the balloting began. By this time, he was sure of 740 of the 761 votes needed for nomination.

The party bosses were still against nominating Kennedy. The very efficiency of his organization frightened them. He was independent. He had made no commitments. They hoped he could be stopped on the first ballot. If that happened, a compromise candidate might be chosen. But they knew that if he had as many as 700 votes, he probably could not be stopped.

On Wednesday, the day of the nomination, the frenzied, screaming supporters of Stevenson swarmed around the Arena carrying their signs and chanting their songs. Partly by trickery, they managed to get into the Arena and fill the galleries. But in spite of their noisy enthusiasm, the Stevenson followers represented only a few votes among the delegates.

Bob Kennedy was determined that his brother be nominated on the first ballot. "If we don't win tonight, we're dead," he said to his aides as the presidential nominating speeches began.

First to be nominated was Lyndon Johnson, by Sam Rayburn of Texas, the Speaker of the House. He had been the permanent chairman of the Democratic convention a number of times. This year he had refused the post so that he could nominate Johnson.

Orville Freeman, the Governor of Minnesota, nominated Kennedy. Until the last, Kennedy had hoped that Stevenson would nominate him and thus declare himself, but Stevenson refused to be committed.

Senator Eugene McCarthy of Minnesota nominated Stevenson in one of the finest speeches of the convention. "Do not reject this man who has made us all proud to be Democrats," he pleaded. "Do not leave this prophet without honor in his own country." .

The convention hall almost exploded after McCarthy's speech. Stevenson supporters poured out of the galleries and onto the floor. "We want Stevenson!" was their overwhelming cry. At last the chairman ordered the lights to be turned out to restore order.

Kennedy and those closest to him were watching the convention on television in his hideaway apartment near the convention hall. The little group kept tally of the votes. Twice the television screen went black as a fuse was blown, to the frantic dismay of those who were watching. Then the air conditioner was turned off and there was no more trouble.

The balloting began.

"Alabama!" shouted the clerk.

"Alabama casts twenty votes for Johnson; three and a half for Kennedy; one half for Stevenson; three and a half for Symington."

State after state called out its vote. Slowly the vote for Kennedy mounted. All along there were a few more for Kennedy than Bob Kennedy had expected, and a few less for Johnson. At last came Wisconsin. When the vote was cast, Kennedy had 748 votes. Only 13 more were needed for him to win. Wyoming would be next.

"There's Ted talking to the chairman," said the candidate. "This could do it." Wyoming was the last state to vote, but the territories that would follow would surely make up the needed 13 votes. Wyoming had planned to give only a portion of its votes to Kennedy. But Ted Kennedy pointed out to the chairman the important role his state could now play at the convention.

The chairman rose. "Wyoming casts all fifteen votes for John F. Kennedy, the next President of the United States," he shouted. It was all over. Kennedy had been nominated on the first ballot.

First Kennedy telephoned his wife, who had remained at Hyannis Port. Then, with the sirens of police cars screaming to clear the way, Kennedy and his party drove to the Sports Arena. On the way, on bits of paper, he scribbled notes on the brief speech he would make.

When at last the convention crowd had begun to leave, Kennedy and his party returned to his hideaway apartment. There, a weary but happy candidate and his friends ate scrambled eggs and toast.

Who should be the candidate for the Vice-Presidency? There were only twenty-four hours in which to make a choice. Some thought Kennedy probably would have preferred Hubert Humphrey, but Humphrey had come out in support of Stevenson. Others were thought of as well.

But Lyndon B. Johnson seemed the logical choice, in spite of the harsh remarks he had made about Kennedy during the campaign for nomination. Kennedy had come out strongly in favor of the civil rights plank in the platform. This stand would make it harder for him to win the votes of Democrats in the South. Johnson could do much to carry that part of the country for the Democratic party.

Early Thursday morning, Kennedy called the Johnson hotel suite and asked for an interview with the Senator. About ten o'clock in the morning, the two men met and discussed the proposal. Johnson asked time to think about it.

"I'll call you in two or three hours," said Kennedy. He was amazed that Johnson was considering the matter favorably. He had expected a refusal.

While awaiting the telephone call, Johnson consulted his advisers. Johnson had arguments for and against acceptance. The position of Vice-President was not nearly as important as being Majority Leader in the Senate. On the other hand, being Vice-President

John Kennedy (left), Adlai Stevenson (center), and Lyndon Johnson before presidential balloting, Los Angeles, 1960.

would make Johnson a national leader rather than only a representative of his state.

There was much telephoning and discussion on both sides, for many of the followers of both men were against the choice. Late in the afternoon, however, the arrangements were completed, and Johnson was nominated by acclamation on Thursday night.

Late Friday afternoon, John F. Kennedy appeared before a crowd of eighty thousand people at the Los Angeles Coliseum, formally to accept the nomination. On the platform with him were all the members of his family except his wife and his father. Jacqueline Kennedy was expecting a baby and so had not attended the convention. Ambassador Kennedy had quietly left on a plane for New York that morning. He knew that there was strong feeling against him and planned to keep in the background while his son was campaigning.

"The old era is ending, the old ways will not do," said Kennedy in his acceptance speech. "We stand today on the edge of a new frontier. The new frontier of which I speak is a set of challenges. They sum up not what I intend to offer the American people, but what I intend to ask of them."

The crowd cheered. They offered their help. They promised their votes for the "New Frontier."

6

THE PRESIDENTIAL CAMPAIGN WAS ON. It promised to be a hard race. Both candidates planned extensive tours of the country. Richard Nixon was able to start campaigning soon after his nomination for the Presidency by the Republican Party. Kennedy had to remain in Washington for a special session of Congress and was not able to start until Labor Day.

Throughout the campaign, Kennedy sought to win the support of the people in the large cities because of their heavy vote in the electoral college. He did not do as well as Nixon in the farm areas. Nixon by nature and background was able to speak to the farmers in a manner that was more to their liking than Kennedy's, with his elegance of manner and Harvard accent.

Wildly cheering crowds swarmed around Kennedy wherever he went. Young people especially turned out to greet him. His hands were raw and bruised sometimes from handshaking. Girls took to jumping up and down and shrieking wildly when he came into sight. "If the voting age would be changed to nine, I'd win in every state," he said.

His main theme in every talk was, "We must get this country moving again," and he emphasized, "We must restore our lost prestige." His voice was rasping at first, and he spoke with the broad *a* of the Harvard accent. He was usually serious and intent, emphasizing his words with a chopping motion of his right hand or a pointed finger. Occasionally there were bits of irony and wit, but never high-sounding political oratory. People began to talk about the "Kennedy style" in political speeches. "The sixties are going to be different," he promised. "We are a new generation."

Ted Sorenson and Arthur Schlesinger, Jr., a Harvard professor and Pulitzer Prize winner for biography, were among the gifted writers who worked on the speeches. Often, however, Kennedy departed from the prepared text and added phrases of his own. His speeches had his own style and ideas. The main job of the staff was to gather statistics and information.

As usual, all the members of the Kennedy family worked in the campaign. Even Jackie Kennedy, though she was expecting a baby, met groups of women at weekly teas. She also went with her husband to some of the places on his campaign tour. Where the background of the people was French or Spanish, she did much to win voters by speaking to them in the language of their ancestors.

Senator and Mrs. Kennedy campaigning in New York City, 1960.

All of the Kennedys with the exception of Rosemary were married now, and the in-laws also helped in the campaign. In most cases, the Kennedys had chosen husbands or wives who, like themselves, were wealthy, athletic, and dedicated to public service.

From childhood on, Rosemary had never been able to compete with her sisters and brothers. She was sweet and attractive but slow to develop. The family had realized in time that Rosemary was mentally retarded.

For a long time, however, her parents refused to send her to an institution. At last, the Kennedys accepted the fact that Rosemary would be better off away from her family. After much consideration, when she was twenty-three, she was sent to a special school in Wisconsin. Eventually, the Kennedys quieted rumors by making a public statement about Rosemary. The family also contributed millions of dollars to this cause. The condition of Rosemary Kennedy, however, was one point that was never mentioned in the campaign of 1960.

One incident in the campaign did much to win the votes of Negroes for Kennedy. On October 24, a Georgia Policeman arrested Dr. Martin Luther King, a Negro leader of the civil rights movement in the South, for a traffic violation. Feeling against the Negroes was high in Georgia, and Mrs. King was afraid that her husband might be dragged from the jail and lynched. When this was brought to Kennedy's attention, he telephoned Mrs. King and expressed his sympathy and desire to help her husband. Later Robert Kennedy telephoned the Georgia judge and succeeded in having Dr. King released on bail.

As a result, King's father, who was a Baptist minister with a large following, said that he was going to vote for Kennedy even though Kennedy was a Catholic. This decision did much to influence the votes of Negroes in other parts of the country.

Kennedy had hoped that the primary in West Virginia had settled the religious issue, but he was wrong. As the campaign went on, from all over the country, he had evidence that many people were fearful of having

73

a Catholic for President. He therefore accepted an invitation to speak at a meeting in Houston, Texas, of Protestant clergymen.

On the evening of September 12, Kennedy addressed three hundred ministers gathered at the Rice Hotel in Houston. All during the weekend, he and Ted Sorenson, a Unitarian, had studied what he should say. "We can win or lose the election right here in Houston," Sorenson told a friend.

The ministers were courteous but somewhat hostile as Kennedy began his speech. It was short and in his best style.

Senator Kennedy campaigning in Brooklyn, Illinois, 1960.

"I believe in an America where the separation of church and state is absolute—where no Catholic prelate would tell the President, should he be a Catholic, how to act, and no Protestant minister would tell his parishioners for whom to vote," he told them.

After this, he gave his views on religion and stated what his position had been as a Senator and would be if he were elected President. Following the speech, the ministers asked questions both on Kennedy's actions in the past and possible situations in the future. In the end, Kennedy stated firmly that if elected President, if he found any conflict between his conscience and the Presidency, he would resign that office.

The statements were clear and without any reservations. By the end of the meeting, Kennedy had won the respect and friendship of many who were present. Parts of the program were nationally televised. It was filmed and used by the Democrats on many occasions. How much effect the meeting had on the attitude of people throughout the nation cannot be told, but Kennedy felt better himself for having faced the issue.

Another important campaign development came when for the first time in history, the two major candidates were scheduled for a series of debates on television. By 1960, most families had television in their homes. More voters could see and hear the candidates for themselves than had ever been possible before.

The representatives for Nixon and Kennedy met in September to discuss conditions. The plans were finally made. The first debate was to be in the CBS studio in Chicago on September 26. The other three were evenly spaced throughout October.

In the first debate, Kennedy was the first to speak. Although usually he had nervous mannerisms when he was under stress, he seemed calm and at ease as he spoke. He wore a dark blue suit which showed up well against the light background curtain behind him.

Nixon's light gray suit almost faded into the gray of the background curtain. He had lost weight and looked gaunt and tired. His face looked heavy and bearded in spite of the light makeup he had been given. He suffered from the heat of the television lights. Perspiration showed as he spoke, though at his request, the cameramen were careful not to show him as he mopped his brow. Kennedy seemed cool and composed.

But it was not only the contrast in the appearance of the two men that dismayed the Republicans as they watched, but what they had to say. The opening debate was confined to the domestic issues, and Kennedy spoke to the nation on his views. Nixon instead answered Kennedy's statements, and in most cases said

Senator Kennedy (left), Vice President Richard Nixon (right) engage in televised debate, October, 1960. NBC's Frank McGee moderates.

that he agreed with his opponent. This "me-too" attitude astounded his followers. They had expected a fighting Nixon. Instead he seemed weak and indecisive. Kennedy amazed his listeners with his knowledge of facts and the latest statistics.

There was no question that Kennedy had won in this first debate. Up to this time, Nixon and his supporters had attacked Kennedy as being too young and inexperienced for the office of President. Now Nixon was the one who looked immature and incapable.

The debates were the turning point in the campaign. In surveys that were made, it was learned that over 115 million people had watched the debates. This was the greatest television audience in our history.

About 70 million had watched the first debate. In a survey made of the voters after the election, 57 percent of them stated that the debates had influenced their votes. Another 6 percent said that their final decision was determined by the debates. "It was TV more than anything else that turned the tide," said Kennedy in a press conference after the election.

The election was on November 8, 1960. Bob Kennedy's house at Hyannis Port was the headquarters for the Kennedy family and workers on election day. First to report were the big cities, and at ten o'clock, Kennedy seemed way ahead. Then the trend changed as returns came in from the rural areas, especially in the Midwest and West. Slowly the troubled watchers went to bed, except for Bob Kennedy who stayed at the telephone. Jack Kennedy was one of the last to leave.

"This will probably not be decided until morning," he said to his brother. "I think I'll get some sleep. Let me know if you hear anything." Then he calmly left the room.

At dawn, victory, though a very narrow one, was assured for John F. Kennedy. Almost 69 million people had voted, the highest number on record. Kennedy had a majority of only about 112,000 votes, the closest election in seventy-six years.

In the early afternoon, a motorcade drove from the

Kennedy compound to the Hyannis Port Armory, which had been the election headquarters for the public. This time Joe Kennedy was on the platform.

In a brief speech, the President-elect read the telegrams of congratulation he had received from Nixon and President Eisenhower. At the end of his speech, he said, "My wife and I now prepare for a new administration—and a new baby."

Kennedy was exhausted after the election, and went immediately to his father's house at Palm Beach for a much-needed rest. However, his days were work-filled. There were only about ten weeks before inauguration, and much had to be done.

Kennedy's most important and pressing job was to select his Cabinet. It was a far more difficult task than he had expected. "I thought this part of being President was going to be fun," he remarked with a groan as he studied hundreds of documents and interviewed countless people.

Frequently in the past, Cabinet members had been appointed for political reasons. Kennedy was determined, however, that ability to do the job would be his first consideration for the office. "I don't care if the men selected are Democrats, Republicans, or Igorots," he remarked.

The most important appointments were the Secretaries of State, Treasury, and Defense. Adlai Stevenson seemed the most logical choice for State, and it was an appointment that he wanted. But Kennedy thought that the Senate would not approve the appointment. He decided to make Stevenson the Ambassador to the United Nations. He would make his best contribution there, as he was well thought of in foreign countries.

Kennedy appointed Dean Rusk as Secretary of State. He had been in the State Department under George Marshall during the Truman administration, and was now President of the Rockefeller Foundation.

Robert S. McNamara, recently made president of the Ford Motor Company, was appointed Secretary of Defense. McNamara had always been a Republican, but had voted for Kennedy in the 1960 election. He knew the technique of managing business on a big scale, and he thought this same technique could be used in the business of government.

Douglas Dillon, also a Republican and Undersecretary of State in the Eisenhower administration, was made Secretary of the Treasury. In spite of his political background, Kennedy thought that Dillon was highly qualified for the position because of his banking experience.

Other men, equally qualified, were given appointments. Governor Orville Freeman of Minnesota became Secretary of Agriculture. Arthur Goldberg, a brilliant lawyer and negotiator for the labor unions, became Secretary of Labor. Abraham Ribicoff, Governor of Connecticut, became Secretary of Health, Education, and Welfare. Luther H. Hodges, former Governor of North Carolina, and now a businessman, became Secretary of Commerce. Stewart L. Udall, who had served for six years in Congress, became Secretary of the Interior.

The most difficult appointment for Kennedy to make was that of his brother Robert as Attorney General. There was a rare bond of understanding and confidence between the two brothers. They had always worked closely together, and Kennedy wanted his brother to have access to the White House at all times. A cabinet post was the only solution. Robert Kennedy was reluctant to take the post, mainly because there would be criticism that the family had too much power. For two weeks he worried about whether he should accept the position. All his mature life he had worked for his brother, and he wanted to continue to do so. In addition, their father felt that not only should Bob be near Jack, but that he deserved the appointment for the work he had done in the campaign. In the end, Robert Kennedy agreed to be the Attorney General.

Dr. Janet Travell of New York was made White House physician. She was the first woman to be given that post, but Kennedy liked the treatments she had prescribed for his back. It was Dr. Travell who had recommended that he sit as much as possible in a rocking chair.

Ted Sorenson was especially pleased with the appointments. All of the men, he thought, were "sacrificing" in order to come to Washington, but accepting the appointments because they were needed.

Newspapermen thought Kennedy was unduly slow about announcing his appointments. They did not realize how much time and thought he was putting

President-elect, Mrs. Kennedy, and their son John F., Jr., 1960.

into the task. Most of the announcements were made from the doorstep of the Kennedy house in Georgetown. It was one of the coldest winters in Washington, and the throngs of reporters waited in the bitter cold each day until the President-elect came out in the frosty air to announce a new appointment.

There was a special reason why Kennedy was in Washington now, though he was tanned and rested and had gained fifteen pounds. It was to be near his wife. The Kennedys had spent a quiet Thanksgiving in their Georgetown home. That evening, Kennedy had left for Palm Beach, as the birth of their child was not expected for several weeks. As soon as Kennedy's plane landed at Palm Beach, he was told there was a telephone call for him. His wife had been taken to the hospital. The baby was being born before the date expected. The party went right back. Then on the airplane's radio came the good news of the birth of the baby.

"Mrs. Kennedy has given birth to a boy. Mother and child are doing well," the press secretary announced to the reporters. The new baby was named John F. Kennedy, Jr.

There were eight inches of snow in Washington, the day before the inauguration of John F. Kennedy. The streets were brilliant with sunshine on Inauguration Day. In spite of the bitter cold, the grandstands and sidewalks were crowded with people. Somehow Pennsylvania Avenue had been cleared of snow for the parade.

Kennedy and his wife went to the White House for coffee and a pleasant visit with the Eisenhowers before driving to the Capital. Although Kennedy had not come home until four in the morning from a party given in his honor by his father, the President-elect had risen early to attend Mass at Holy Trinity Church in Washington.

The inauguration ceremonies were brief. Cardinal Cushing of Boston, who had married the Kennedys and baptized their children, gave the invocation. Robert Frost, the New England poet, read part of a poem he had written for the occasion. The old man could not finish the reading, because the glare from the snow and sun blinded him, so he recited from memory something else he had written.

At 12:51, Chief Justice Warren administered the oath of office. Hatless and without an overcoat, John F. Kennedy placed his hand on the Fitzgerald family Bible and repeated the oath. Then he began his address. He had thought about it and rephrased it many times, and made small changes even at the end. He had wanted it to be the shortest inauguration address of the twentieth century. It took only fourteen minutes to deliver, but it has become almost a classic in our language.

As he had frequently done during his campaign, the new President addressed most of his words to young people. "Let the word go forth from this time and place," he cried, "to friend and foe alike, that the torch has been passed to a new generation of Americans."

There were sacrifices that he called on them to make. "My fellow Americans," he concluded, "ask not what your country can do for you—ask what you can do for your country."

President Kennedy delivering his inaugural address, January, 1961.

After lunch, the inauguration parade began, and the President sat in the reviewing stand and waved and smiled through the whole parade. That night, there were five inaugural balls, and President Kennedy attended them all, though Mrs. Kennedy, who was still not very strong after John's birth, left after attending two.

When it was almost dawn, President Kennedy came back to the White House. He ran up the steps, then turned to wave and smile to the waiting reporters and photographers. The new administration had begun.

7

FIVE DAYS AFTER HIS INAUGURATION, President Kennedy had his first televised press conference. During the campaign, the President and his advisers had learned that his style of speaking was exactly right for television. He spoke simply. He made few gestures. He had a sincerity and charm which could be seen on television, though they were lost at times in a great public gathering. Through television, the President felt he could speak directly to the people. In this way his words and ideas would not be changed by a reporter's account.

The televised press conferences continued. They occurred every two or three weeks and were announced well in advance. Efforts were made to have them at a time that did not conflict with popular programs. For hours before each meeting, the President worked with his staff in an effort to prepare for any questions that might be asked. He constantly amazed those who watched and listened by his ready response to questions and his wit and ease of manner.

Kennedy's relations with the press were usually

friendly. His natural ability to read quickly was increased by a speed-reading course he had taken when he was a Senator. He read many of the daily newspapers and the current event magazines, and would tell a reporter when he liked the way an event was reported or when a story was well-written. He was just as quick, however, to express his displeasure when he thought he had not been given fair treatment in the press. Like all Presidents, he was sensitive to criticism.

Lyndon B. Johnson as Vice-President was loyal at all times to President Kennedy. Though he did not always agree with the President, the Vice-President did what he could to back Kennedy's program. In turn, the President did everything he could to lend dignity and importance to Johnson's position. The President was grateful for the help Johnson had given him in the campaign.

In addition, he admired and respected Johnson, and valued his opinion. There had been bitter things said by Johnson about Kennedy before the Democratic convention, but this was over now for the President. Robert Kennedy, however, had not forgotten the comments, and there was some tension between him and the Vice-President.

Johnson was made chairman of various committees. When he was in the United States, he was present at every important policy meeting. The President sent him on goodwill tours to thirty-three countries, an assignment which the Vice-President enjoyed very much.

However, Johnson, like most political leaders who become Vice-President, was not happy in his office. His special talent at getting bills through Congress was not used. He probably missed the importance he had enjoyed when he was Majority Leader. The President knew that Johnson was a proud and sensitive man, and sometimes he found it difficult to write or speak to him. On the whole, however, there was harmony and co-operation between them.

The President's days were work-filled. Usually he was in his office by eight-thirty, having scanned most of the newspapers while he was eating breakfast. The Oval Office of the President was in the west wing of the White House. It was a spacious room with tall French windows overlooking the Rose Garden. The windows had three inches of laminated glass, should any would-be assassin take aim at the chief executive. The staff members had their offices nearby, and they usually had easy access to the President.

The President's desk was one Mrs. Kennedy had discovered in the White House basement. It was an elaborately carved oak desk made from the timbers of the British ship *Resolute*. It had been presented to President Hayes by Queen Victoria.

A model of the ship *Constitution* was on the mantel, and naval prints were on the walls. On the President's desk were beautifully bound copies of the books he had written, and the coconut shell he had sent with the natives at the time of the sinking of his PT boat.

Kennedy enjoyed being able to look out into the Rose Garden. There had been only a few rose bushes in it when Kennedy took office. He soon ordered flowers that were in season planted in a rectangle around a small lawn. He delighted in the garden and frequently walked in it, or checked on the flower beds as he walked to his office from the mansion, for he loved being outdoors. The garden also became a place where he greeted dignitaries or special groups.

There were youth and good times in the White House now. Both Mrs. Truman and Mrs. Eisenhower had rarely entertained except for certain social affairs that had become customary. But the Kennedys were young. They were wealthy and used to international society. Not since the time of Dolly Madison had there been so much gaiety and lavish hospitality in the White House.

Name bands furnished music for dancing in the East Room. The parties lasted until the early hours of the morning. As much as possible, guests were chosen because the Kennedys wanted them, not because of their prominence. The President moved sociably from group to group, usually with a half-finished glass of champagne in his hand. He did not drink very much, and he rarely danced. But everyone felt that John Kennedy was enjoying the party and was personally pleased to see each guest. The state dinners occurred as always, but Mrs. Kennedy's gift for mingling with people and the menus provided by her French chef, Henri Verdun, made them cheerful as well as elegant affairs.

But the special entertainments planned by the Kennedys were the social events that were remem-

President Kennedy (left) and Mrs. Kennedy at White House party.

bered. People with talent were favored guests at the White House. The Kennedys gave a reception to honor the winners of the Nobel Prize. Other talented people in arts and literature were honored guests. A special stage was devised for the East Room so that performances of the ballet and of Shakespeare could be given.

Life in Washington was influenced by the New Frontier. People became more interested in the arts because of Mrs. Kennedy's liking for good music, fine paintings, the theater and ballet, and the best in literature. Because the Kennedys liked vigorous sports, there was an emphasis on physical fitness and all kinds of outdoor games.

The President spent more time now than ever before with his own family. They rented a home in the Virginia countryside for weekends and later built a home. They usually had lunch and dinner together. Mrs. Kennedy and the children frequently came into the Oval Office to see the President. There were many public affairs in which she took part with her husband.

Kennedy loved children, and he wanted to be with his own as much as possible. Caroline, who was four years old now, and John, when he learned to walk, came into his bedroom each morning while he ate breakfast and usually walked to the office with him.

Mrs. Kennedy wanted their children to lead as

normal a life as possible. She arranged to have a nursery school on the third floor of the White House so that Caroline could go to school with children of her own age. She tried to take them to parks and other places of recreation, though this was difficult because of the publicity connected with their every movement.

Perhaps Mrs. Kennedy's best-known contribution to the administration of her husband was the change she brought about in the public section of the White House. When she was eleven years old, she had been taken on a tour of the White House by her mother. All she remembered was that the crowd shuffled through the rooms. "They didn't even have a booklet to tell you about things," she said later.

Mrs. Kennedy was determined now to make the White House a living museum so that the people could see the history of the nation as they were taken through the rooms. Her first task was to get Congress to pass a bill so that the White House could be designated as a museum. In this way wealthy people could give gifts of rare furnishings, or money to buy these, and they would be retained in the White House.

The bill was passed, and Mrs. Kennedy was not disappointed in the results. People presented to the White House china, furniture, or other things which had been used by earlier Presidents or were genuine antiques from various periods in American history. Money also was donated, and funds were raised by the sale of a beautifully illustrated guide book. Mrs. Kennedy, who herself was an expert on antiques, worked tirelessly with her committee. In February, 1962, she took the nation on a televised tour of the White House and won nationwide approval of what she had done.

President Kennedy was proud of his wife's achievements. He appeared on the television program to say so, and congratulated her when the number of tourists almost doubled in the first year of his administration.

The President himself was busy with bigger problems, trying some new approaches. In his first State of the Union message, President Kennedy asked for the creation of a "Peace Corps." He had suggested the idea in his campaign, and he wanted to put it into effect as soon as possible. Peace meant more than just an absence of war, he said. World peace might be achieved if there was less dissatisfaction among people because of ignorance, poverty, and disease. The President was confident that there would be many volunteers for the program.

The Peace Corps was organized on March 1, 1961. It was made up of youthful volunteers for the most part, though many retired persons were in the program. Their purpose was to bring American skill to the people of less modern nations. The volunteers received only a small salary. They lived like the people of the host country, learned their language, and helped them to develop their resources. They pledged themselves to be non-political.

As President Kennedy predicted, the Peace Corps was successful. The number of volunteers went from 500 to 10,000 by 1964, and they were working in forty-six countries. The members taught school, worked with farmers, helped construct buildings, taught trades and new methods of doing things, and so on. In time, al-

President Kennedy's first Cabinet session. From left: Postmaster General Edward Day; UN Ambassador Adlai Stevenson; Vice President Johnson; Defense Secretary Robert McNamara; Agriculture Secretary Orville Freeman; Labor Secretary Arthur Goldberg; Health, Education, and Welfare Secretary Abraham Ribicoff; Commerce Secretary Luther Hodges; Attorney General Robert Kennedy; Secretary of State Dean Rusk; President Kennedy; Treasury Secretary Douglas Dillon; and Interior Secretary Stewart Udall, January, 1961.

though the Corps had been ridiculed at first, it won general approval.

The members of the Peace Corps brought back to this country an understanding of the problems of other parts of the world. In time, they became better known to the people of the countries they lived in than our diplomats. The Peace Corps was the achievement in which President Kennedy took the greatest pride and satisfaction.

During the campaign of 1960, Kennedy had promised to improve the relations between the countries of Latin America and the United States. He meant this sincerely. The "Good Neighbor" policy of President Roosevelt had declined in recent years. The Latin American countries were bitter now in their attitude toward their neighbor to the north. This feeling was shown when Vice-President Nixon had visited Caracas, Venezuela, and was stoned and spat upon in a parade through the streets.

On March 13, 1961, President Kennedy invited the Latin American diplomats to meet with him in the White House. In his speech, he called on all the people of the hemisphere to join in a new "Alliance for Progress" to satisfy the needs of the Latin American people for work, homes, land, and education. "If countries of Latin America are ready to do their part, the United

States will provide the resources," he promised.

The audience was deeply moved by the President's understanding and his program to help solve their problems. "We have not had such words since the days of Roosevelt," said the Ambassador from Venezuela.

The first presidential trip to Latin America was in December, 1961. Caracas, Venezuela, and Bogota, Colombia, were the cities visited. There were anxious times in the State Department as the trip was planned because of the treatment that had been given three years before to Vice-President Nixon.

The reception of the Kennedys was quite different. Mrs. Kennedy, who had been practicing her Spanish, went with her husband. Wildly cheering crowds greeted them, and they were showered with pink confetti instead of stones.

Each year after that, President Kennedy went to Latin America. He always received an enthusiastic welcome, though he was disappointed that there was so little progress made in improving the living conditions of the people.

On April 11, 1961, the attention of the world was caught when Russia sent Yuri Gagarin into orbit around the earth. He was the first man to go into space. The success of the Russians was a shock to the American people. There was an immediate cry for action by our government. The President summoned the various heads of our space program to a meeting at the White House. "Is there any way in which we can catch up to Russia?" he asked.

The answers of some of the scientists were vague and not very encouraging. The Russians were far ahead of us in the development of big rockets, the President was told. Our smaller space instruments gave us far better scientific information, but it would take a big rocket to get to the moon.

"How long would it take to overcome the Russians?" the President asked. "Would the gain in prestige be worth the billions that must be spent?" Again he had only vague answers from some of those he questioned.

There were other scientists who thought we could be first if we had the will and the desire to be ahead. The cost, however, would be tremendous. We would have to spend 20 to 40 billion dollars in the next ten years, and there was no guarantee of success.

President Kennedy had always been willing to accept a challenge. Six weeks later, he addressed Congress for the second time in his administration. It was "time for a great new American enterprise," he stated. Then he told about the cost and the problems involved.

"If we are to go only halfway, it would be better not to go at all. I believe we should go to the moon."

On May 5, 1961, Alan B. Shepard made the first successful flight into space for the United States. The flight took only fifteen minutes as against the hour and a half of Gagarin's flight. But it had been done in the open with the whole world watching on television. From that time on, the United States was firmly in the race for space. Late in February, 1962, Colonel John R. Glenn made three successful orbits around the earth. President Kennedy went to Cape Canaveral (now Cape Kennedy) to pay tribute to the astronaut.

Another problem President Kennedy had to deal with in the first months of his administration was the planned invasion of Cuba by Cuban refugees in this

President Kennedy and Colonel John Glenn at Cape Canaveral, Florida.

country and Central America. On November 18, 1960, just ten days after his election, President-elect Kennedy for the first time was told of a dramatic secret plan. The United States was helping some Cuban refugees in their preparations to invade their country and overthrow the rule of Fidel Castro.

A Cuban brigade was being trained in Guatemala. The United States had guaranteed to train, equip, and advise the force, but not to intervene directly with troops or air power. As later events showed, the Cubans either did not understand or believe that American armed forces would not take part in their invasion. Our program to help them was under the Central Intelligence Agency (CIA).

President Kennedy agreed to continue with the program, and the training went on. The plan was well underway, and Kennedy, new in the Presidency, was reluctant to challenge experts who favored the plan. By April, 1961, the Cuban forces were eager to carry out their invasion. In addition, the government of Guatemala informed the United States that the Cuban brigade would have to be withdrawn from Guatemala by the end of the month.

The plan of the CIA and the Cubans was to invade Cuba at the Bay of Pigs. Two days before the invasion, B26 planes supplied by the United States but manned by Cuban pilots were to fly from Nicaragua and attack Castro's air force. At the time of the landing on the beaches, there was to be a second air attack.

If the invasion went off as planned, the Americans in charge of the plan thought there would be a general uprising of discontented people in Cuba. If the plan failed, they told Kennedy, the invaders could retreat to the mountains and from there, make guerrilla attacks until their purpose was achieved.

President Kennedy now had frequent meetings with those he considered best able to advise him. The Joint Chiefs of Staff, the heads of the CIA, Secretaries Rusk and McNamara in the Cabinet, and leaders in Congress discussed the plan with him. All thought it would succeed. Only Senator Fulbright and Chester Bowles of the State Department did not agree, but mainly because they thought we had no right to be involved.

On Monday, April 17, the invading forces landed at dawn at the Bay of Pigs. Two days before, the first air flight from Nicaragua had taken place as planned. However, only five of Castro's planes had been destroyed. The world soon guessed the United States was involved. There had been such worldwide criticism of the part played by the United States in this first air strike that the President had ordered the cancellation of the second air strike. At the time, he did not know the true military situation. Castro's forces and equipment were much stronger than anyone had thought. Many later believed the invasion was doomed to failure by the lack of air strength of the invaders.

Castro's intelligence forces had learned what the invaders had planned. He was ready for them when they landed at the Bay of Pigs. In a short time, his air force sank two of the ships carrying ammunition and means of communication. With the news of this, President Kennedy ordered the second air strike by Cuban pilots, but he still refused to give the landing forces air cover by planes from the United States. Kennedy did not want the United States to get into a full war with Cuba. Russia might come to fight for Cuba, and we would be in a terrible world war. He still believed the plan would succeed.

On Wednesday, the survivors of the Cuban brigade surrendered to Castro's forces and were taken to prison. The invasion had failed. There had been no general uprising of the people, for there was no leadership or organization of a resistance movement in Cuba. Nor could the invaders retreat to the mountains, for they were too far away. Besides, Castro's police had strong control of Cuba, making both a general uprising and gathering of troops in the mountains impossible.

Kennedy had been misinformed.

In Washington, Kennedy sat with his advisers to see what could be done. Slowly he began to realize what was the root of the trouble. He had accepted the advice of men whom he had thought were experts. Much of the blame lay on the CIA, which had been confident of success and had given him faulty information. He saw that a small invasion, the kind that had been tried, could not have succeeded. A larger invasion involving the United States would have brought the world dangerously close to war. He regretted not cancelling the whole plan in the beginning. At least, he thought, he should have put it off until he had a chance to study it more. As one of his aides said later, "The President asked the right questions. He got the wrong answers."

So far there was little known by the general public about what had happened, for there were no reporters with the expedition. On Thursday, Kennedy spoke at a meeting of the American Society of Editors. "The President and the editors in a democracy have an obligation to the people to present the facts," he said. "With that obligation in mind, I have decided to discuss briefly the recent events in Cuba." Then he stated what had happened. He accepted the full blame for the failure of the expedition.

Kennedy consulted former President Eisenhower and other influential Republicans who were likely to criticize his policies. He told them frankly about his mistakes in judgment, and asked for their advice and help. This did much to bring national unity and lessen some of the bitter criticism. He appointed Robert Kennedy and others to make a thorough investigation of the whole Cuban affair. Later, Castro released those taken prisoner. Kennedy was greatly moved when the men presented him with their brigade banner which had flown on the beach at the time of the invasion.

In spite of the fact that the plan for the invasion

President Kennedy and Former President Eisenhower confer at Camp David, Maryland, 1961.

of Cuba had been made in President Eisenhower's administration, President Kennedy was blamed for the failure. He was accused of being too hesitant, and of dooming the invasion by making changes at the last minute. However, in a poll taken after the Bay of Pigs incident, it was shown that 82 percent of the people approved of the Kennedy administration. The people seemed to sympathize with the young President and wish him well in his office.

But the Cuban affair had taught Kennedy many things. Never again would he depend solely on those who should be experts. He must also have the advice of the people he had worked with the longest, whom he knew best and could trust most.

Though the opponents of President Kennedy never ceased to criticize the Bay of Pigs affair, the general criticism ended. The newspapers were soon filled with accounts of the impending visit of the President to Europe. A meeting between Kennedy and General de Gaulle, the French head of state, was scheduled for June, 1961. Mrs. Kennedy would accompany her husband.

Then it was announced that the President would go from France to Vienna to meet with Nikita Khrushchev, the Soviet Premier. Kennedy hoped in his meeting with Khrushchev to discuss the relationship between East and West Germany as well as the problem of the neutrality of Laos.

Those close to Kennedy knew that he wanted to look at Khrushchev, to hear him talk, and to watch him across the conference table. It was thought that Khrushchev also wanted to see the new President of the United States. "Much of what the Soviets do is based on Khrushchev's opinion of the leaders," our Ambassador to Russia told the President.

In the final week before his departure, Kennedy devoted most of his time to studying the leaders he was to meet. Their speeches and memoirs, as well as articles about them, were read. Men who had talked at length to Khrushchev or been our ambassadors were interviewed. Never before had there been such preparation for an international visit.

The Kennedys left for France on May 29. Their reception in Paris was triumphal. De Gaulle and his wife met them at the airport, and there was much colorful display. Cheering crowds lined the streets as the motorcade moved slowly along.

There were friendly talks for the next few days between the leaders, and much lavish entertainment. Most significant was an evening spent at the Palace of Versailles. There was a candlelit dinner in the Hall of Mirrors followed by a ballet performance in the beautiful Louis XV theater. Then the guests were driven slowly through the gardens at Versailles, their sparkling fountains and glowing flowerbeds illuminated by huge spotlights.

The biggest triumph, however, was the response of the French people to Mrs. Kennedy. Crowds jammed to watch her every move. The newspapers were filled with accounts of her beauty, her charm, and her queenly bearing. Young people were told to imitate these qualities. Her costumes, which were breathtaking even in this center of fashion, were described and pictured in detail.

In her own way, Mrs. Kennedy was able to help her husband. She spoke fluent French, and so she could interpret for him in private conversations with De Gaulle. In her conversations with De Gaulle, who was enchanted with her, she was able to tell him of the views and ability of her husband.

Kennedy laughingly admitted the greater interest of the French people in his wife. "I do not think it inappropriate to introduce myself to this audience," he began his press conference in Paris. "I am the man who accompanied Jacqueline Kennedy to Paris, and I have enjoyed it."

On the morning of June 3, the Kennedys arrived in Vienna. Again the cheering crowds lined the streets, though it was raining. Many more people came than had turned out for Khrushchev the day before.

Shortly after twelve o'clock, Khrushchev came to the American Embassy where the Kennedy party was staying. From that time on, there were eleven hours of meetings between the two leaders. There was also some entertainment, particularly a huge and colorful state dinner at the Schönbrunn Palace.

Khrushchev, too, had prepared for the meeting. "I have read all your speeches," he told Kennedy.

Kennedy soon learned that Khrushchev was well informed. He was agreeable and sometimes told political jokes. Kennedy was witty at times and equally well informed. But the Soviet leader steadily refused to give in on any point except in regard to Laos. This

President Kennedy and Soviet Premier Nikita Khrushchev, Vienna, 1961.

was a small country in Southeast Asia in which there was a civil war as rival powers tried to gain control. Trouble there could involve both Russia and America. Both leaders agreed to work to make Laos a neutral country.

The crucial point of discussion between Khrushchev and Kennedy was in regard to Berlin. After World War II, Germany had been divided into four zones, each controlled by one of the four great powers, Great Britain, France, Russia, and the United States. In time, however, the four zones became two separate republics, East Germany allied with the Russians, and West Germany allied with the other three powers. The city of Bonn became the capital of West Germany.

The important city of Berlin, however, was geographically deep in East Germany. It was divided into east and west sections, with a part of East Germany between West Berlin and the remainder of West Germany. The western powers, however, had the right to have troops stationed in West Berlin and to have access to it from West Germany, even though the route was across territory belonging to East Germany. East and West Berlin went their separate ways, though there was hostility between them.

Shortly after President Kennedy was inaugurated, Khrushchev announced that he intended to make a separate peace treaty with East Germany and thus officially end the war, even if the other three powers refused to sign the treaty. In that case, all of Berlin would come under the control of East Germany. The western position was that a treaty should only be signed with a reunified Germany, with a government chosen by all the people of Germany in free elections. In addition, the U.S. was strongly committed to guarantee the continued freedom of West Berlin.

Now the Russian Premier told Kennedy that a peace treaty between Russia and East Germany would be signed before the end of the year. In reply, Kennedy stated that the western powers were in Berlin legally and would use force to maintain their right to be there "at any risk."

Just before the Americans were leaving, Khrushchev again insisted that his decision to sign a peace treaty with East Germany was "firm." Kennedy looked at him. Neither man smiled. "If that is so," said Kennedy, "it is going to be a cold winter." There were only forced smiles and handshakes for the photographers as the two men parted.

From Vienna, the Americans flew to London where Kennedy conferred briefly with Prime Minister Harold Macmillan of England. The party then returned to the United States.

On June 6, the President broadcast the account of his visit. He had found the meetings with Khrushchev "immensely useful," he said. Both had agreed that Laos should be independent and neutral. But there had been no agreement on Berlin or a treaty to ban nuclear testing. However, "with the will and the work, freedom will prevail," the President assured the people.

Tension concerning Berlin increased during the summer months. Each day about 1500 people left East Berlin to flee to West Berlin. But another 1,000 more were turned back. Then on August 13, at two in the morning, trucks filled with soldiers, workmen, and building material rumbled to the boundary between East and West Berlin. Four hours later, a crude wall of concrete and barbed wire was stretched along most of its length.

President Kennedy addresses the nation on television from the White House on the Berlin Crisis, 1961.

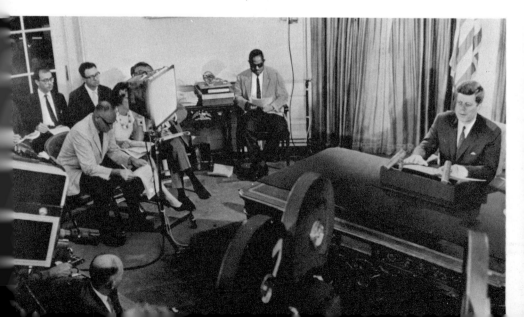

No action was taken either by the United States or West Berlin for several days. In spite of later criticism, it was realized that it would be foolhardy for troops to attempt to break down the wall. It was on the soil of East Berlin. To tear down the wall might have started a war. At the very least, the East Berliners could have built another wall fifty feet back from the first one. It would be better to leave it as a monument to the failure of Communism to hold its people.

President Kennedy, however, sent Vice-President Johnson to West Berlin to assure the West Germans that we would stand firm on our rights and promises to them. We would continue to demand our right to access from West Germany to West Berlin, and to maintain troops in West Berlin.

The test of these rights came a week after the wall was built. We were to send 1500 American troops across the 110 miles of road controlled by the East Germans between West Germany and West Berlin. Johnson remained in West Berlin to greet the troops. Their movement began early in the morning on August 19. The following day, good news came to the White House. The American troops had passed through the Berlin Gate without incident. Lyndon Johnson stayed until the last man went through at eight in the evening.

8

In 1962, President Kennedy was tested by the businessmen of the United States, by the Russians, and by the American people. He won in all three contests.

On April 10, the United States Steel Corporation raised the price of steel by six dollars a ton. By the next day, five other steel companies had also raised their price.

All during the spring, the President had met with the heads of the steel industry and the steelworkers' union to work out a contract between them that would not bring about an increase in the price of steel. Such an increase would be bad for the whole economy of the country. Steel is used in many products—high buildings, automobiles, appliances, bridges, railroads, and so on. If the price of steel would go up, all these commodities would increase in price. As a result, wages would rise in other industries, and prices would continue to climb. The purchasing power of the dollar would go down, and even though wages were higher, less could be bought with the money.

This is inflation. It was the opinion of the President and his advisers that if labor and business leaders were conscientious, we could expand our economy and provide employment without having inflation.

The steelworkers' union had finally accepted a contract with no increase in wages and only a small increase in benefits for the workers. For the steel industry to raise its price only four days after the contract was signed, the President felt, was a breach of faith with him and the union.

The President decided to take his case to the people in a televised press conference. He looked grim as he entered the State Department Auditorium the following day.

"I think he is going to give it to steel," said one reporter who knew the President well.

At once, the President related what had happened

Roger Blough, Board Chairman, U.S. Steel Corp. (left), David J. McDonald, Pres. AFL-CIO United Steel Workers (center), and President Kennedy confer.

and why he considered the action of the steel industry wrong. "The American people will find it hard, as I do, to accept a situation in which a tiny handful of steel executives can show such utter contempt for the interests of 185 million Americans," he said, with unsmiling face and cold, angry eyes.

The public response was in favor of the President's stand. Government statistics that were made public showed that an increase in the price of steel was not needed. The Defense Department announced that it would give contracts only to firms which had not raised prices. One big firm, Inland Steel, said it would wait two weeks before deciding on a price increase. This was the first break in the position of the steel industry. On April 13, Bethlehem Steel withdrew its price increase. By Saturday, the other firms had done the same.

The President was asked if he would "make war" now on industries that did not consider the public interest. "No," said Kennedy. "They are our partners —unwilling partners. I want business to do well, otherwise the government won't do well."

The steel crisis had the result that business leaders felt that the Kennedy administration was against them, in spite of the fact that business was given more help in tax laws and other ways in Kennedy's administration than in Eisenhower's. However, most business leaders were Republicans, and their politics influenced their way of thinking.

The question of Cuba was to come up again before the year was over. Throughout the summer of 1962, Republican leaders broadcast rumors that the Russians were not only sending missiles to Cuba, but experts to build them and fire them. In answer to these charges, the President stated that as far as we knew, the only types of missiles in Cuba were for defensive purposes. He said we had no right to take any action without unquestionable proof of the presence of offensive missiles. He knew that the speakers were probably getting their information from Cuban refugees, and the President doubted if these people were competent to make such judgments.

But he made a public statement that "if Cuba should ever become an offensive military base of significance for the Soviet Union, then this country will do whatever must be done to protect its own security and that of its allies."

Every few days our U2 planes, equipped with cameras, flew at a high altitude over Cuba. On October 14, they took pictures which clearly showed that there was a fast Russian build-up of missiles in Cuba which was far more than defensive. Cloudy weather before this date had obscured the pictures that had been taken. The President ordered that more pictures should be taken. Flights began to be made several times a day.

Kennedy was surprised as well as concerned. He had thought the Russians would not dare to make such a move. "The pictures must be checked and re-checked," he ordered. "There must be no mistake."

For long hours, Kennedy met with his advisers. What should be done? Should Cuba be invaded? Should we tell the Russians to get out— or else? Should we blockade Cuba? Should we take no action at all? The President rejected this suggestion. "The worst course of all would be to do nothing at all," he said.

For the next week, all of the aides and the Cabinet members who were involved met daily with the President. More and more pictures were taken and studied each day. There was no doubt of the intense activity of the Russians in Cuba.

A blockade, the prevention of ships entering Cuba, was considered the best course, though technically this was an act of war. Kennedy thought the blockade would show the world that the United States meant to stand firm, without as great a risk of war as the other actions that had been considered.

Absolute secrecy was maintained by those who met each day. As much as possible, the men tried to

United Nations delegates study photos of Soviet missiles in Cuba, 1962.

lead normal lives and avoid having anyone know so many high officials were having long sessions each day at the White House. The 1962 congressional election was near, and the President himself continued to campaign for certain candidates, though he was in constant touch with those who were meeting. He planned to speak on television on Monday night, October 22, and tell the whole story regarding Cuba to the people. So far, there had been no leak to the public about the situation.

On Monday, before making his speech, the President had notified important leaders in our government and in allied countries of what he intended to say. The Kremlin and the Russian Ambassador in the United States were informed a half hour before the broadcast.

At seven in the evening, all programs were interrupted as the President appeared on television. He told of the buildup of missile sites in Cuba by the Russians. It could not be accepted by this country. To stop it, our government had decided to start a strict blockade of all offensive military equipment going to Cuba, even though this might lead to a nuclear war with Russia.

There was quick approval of the President's action. All the Latin American countries quickly agreed to support the blockade. Nine-tenths of the letters that came to the White House approved.

The blockade went into effect at ten o'clock on Wednesday morning. In the meantime, our various armed forces were making ready for action. There was no doubt of our intention to attack if necessary. Beginning on Tuesday, our planes flew overhead and reported that Russian ships were continuing to move steadily toward Cuba. The whole world waited breathlessly to see what would be the outcome.

Then one by one, the Russian ships made a wide turn and headed back toward Asia. The first test of strength was over. However, the danger was still there, for the Russians continued to work speedily on construction and assembling in Cuba.

On Friday evening, a secret letter came to President Kennedy from Khrushchev. The Russian leader promised that the weapons would be withdrawn from Cuba under the supervision of the United Nations if the United States would end the blockade and guarantee not to invade Cuba. Two days later, Khrushchev stated in a broadcast to the Russian people that the missiles were being withdrawn.

Khrushchev kept his promise. The missiles were gradually taken down and shipped back to Russia, though our Navy closely inspected the cargo of every ship carrying them. In the general approval of President Kennedy's firm stand, the memory of the Bay of Pigs began to fade.

In spite of the fact that the polls showed that the people approved of his administration, John Kennedy knew that the real test of a President's power is his ability to get his program made into law by Congress. The Democratic party had a big majority in Congress, but this did not always help the President. Many of the Democrats were conservatives from the South. A great number of them had voted with the Republicans ever since the days of President Roosevelt. Many of these conservatives controlled the various committees in Congress and could block the President.

Kennedy was not popular with Congress. He had never been one of the cloakroom crowd when he had been a Senator. He had always been independent of his party. Many of the older leaders resented the fact that he had shot past them to the top spot. Others were opposed to him because of his wealth, intellect, and the style of his world. Old timers thought he was advancing too many new ideas; the ideas were coming too fast.

The President submitted many new bills, not because he expected them to be passed, but to get debates, hearings, and public discussion started. In this way the public would be educated, and possibly the bills would be passed in 1964 or 1965.

Kennedy tried to work with Congress. He started the custom of having breakfasts on Tuesday morning with the Democratic leaders in Congress. He liked Carl Albert and Everett Dirksen, the Republican leaders in the House and Senate, and also worked and consulted with them.

The mid-term election would take place on November 6, 1962. All of the members of the House and one-third of the senators are elected every two years, so there is always an election for these offices in the middle of a President's four-year term. The results usually indicate the attitude of the people toward the administration.

Except for 1934, in Roosevelt's first term, every party in power has lost some seats in Congress in this election. Although the 87th Congress had passed 73 out of 107 measures Kennedy had submitted, he was not satisfied. It was a record only surpassed by Roosevelt, but some of Kennedy's most talked-about programs had been defeated. In a number of cases the bill had been defeated only by a few votes. Now in mid-term, the President felt that if some of the conservative members could be replaced by men who were more liberal, perhaps the measures would be passed.

President Kennedy determined to campaign. He loved politics and he liked to campaign. It would be his chance to tell the people about his programs and to draw strength from their response. The election would be the judgment of his administration by the people.

His theme in all his talks was the same. "This country is moving again," he would cry, with the earnest look and chopping gesture of his right hand which had become so familiar. "But we want to finish the job we have started. . . . The Republicans have made the word 'No' a political program. . . . We have lost by such small margins, that we need every vote we can get. Otherwise this country will stand still."

By midnight on election night, President Kennedy thought he had shattered tradition. Instead of losing in the Senate, the Democrats gained four seats, one of which was Massachusetts, won by Edward Kennedy. Only four seats had been lost in the House, and many of those who had been elected were liberals replacing conservatives.

WHEN THE 87TH CONGRESS ended its long session in October 1962, the President had received about half of his requests. Some had been important achievements, but the major bills in which he was most interested had not passed.

Medicare, the bill by which he had hoped to get paid medical care for people over sixty-five, had been bitterly fought by the American Medical Association and had been defeated. His program to give federal aid to education had been lost in a fight over whether it should include parochial as well as public schools.

The President had asked to have taxes reduced. In this way, he thought, more money would be spent for goods, more would be produced, and thus unemployment would be decreased. Many members were horrified by the thought of reducing taxes when we had a huge national debt. The President and his economic advisers reasoned that if more goods were bought and employment was increased, the Treasury actually would take in more money than was lost by reducing taxes.

Another objective of John Kennedy for the second half of his term was to get a treaty with all countries making nuclear weapons to forbid tests of these weapons. At this time, only Russia and the United States were making nuclear weapons, but other countries were planning to do so.

To get the treaty signed, the President had to win agreement not only from Russia, but from our own Senate. All treaties made by the United States have to be ratified by a two-thirds vote of the Senate.

The idea of a ban on nuclear testing had started in the early fifties because of the development of the hydrogen bomb. In 1954, when the first hydrogen bomb was exploded in a test by the United States in the Pacific Ocean near Japan, some Japanese fishermen suffered from burned skin and were very sick. For the first time, the world learned of the terrible effects of radioactive fallout on bones, blood, and unborn children.

Attempts had been made to reach agreement with the Russians about stopping the tests. They failed because we insisted on a large number of inspections at the testing places. The Russians claimed that this would give us a chance to spy on them, and refused to end the testing.

John Kennedy had favored the test ban since

124

1956. He thought the United States should take the lead because we were the only country that had engaged in atomic war in the Second World War. In addition, if testing was stopped, other countries might not attempt to make a bomb. "The weapons of war must be abolished before they abolish us," he said in a speech to the United Nations in 1961.

He had discussed a test ban treaty with Khrushchev when they had met in Vienna. The chief point of argument was still the number of inspections. Khrushchev thought three a year would be enough; Kennedy wanted twenty.

At last on December 19, 1962, Khrushchev wrote Kennedy that Russia would consider a treaty to end nuclear testing provided the United States would agree to only three inspections a year. By this time, our methods of detection were so advanced that it was thought three inspections would be enough.

Averill Harriman was chosen by the President as the man best qualified to negotiate with Khrushchev. He had been our Ambassador to Russia under President Truman and had dealt with Khrushchev. Harriman and Khrushchev and their aides conferred in July, after many exploratory letters and preliminary talks. Finally, they agreed on the terms of a limited test ban treaty.

Flanked by Congressional and diplomatic leaders, President Kennedy signs the Nuclear Test Ban Treaty, 1963.

On July 24, President Kennedy announced this to the people of the United States in a broadcast. "Yesterday," he said, "a shaft of light cut into the darkness." The agreement, he said, would not end all conflict, but it was "an important first step." He ended his speech with the Chinese proverb, "A journey of a thousand miles must begin with a single step." He had said this to Khrushchev in Vienna.

Getting the treaty ratified by the Senate was difficult for the President. Many thought that our national security would be in danger if we did not continue to test our bombs. But John Kennedy thought this treaty was a step toward world peace—"Not merely peace in our time, but peace for all time," he

126

said. "If a world war should come again, all that we have worked for would be destroyed in twenty-four hours." He talked about the treaty every time he spoke in public, trying to convince the people and the Senators.

On September 24, the Senate ratified the treaty by a vote of 80 to 19. Many historians believe that the test ban treaty was the greatest achievement of President Kennedy's administration.

Another important development in the second half of the Kennedy term was the struggle of the Negroes to win civil rights. The first step by the government to end segregation had come during World War II. Men in our armed forces of all colors and races were to be treated equally in the service, though there was still discrimination by civilians. The second and more far-reaching step came in 1954 when the Supreme Court outlawed segregation in the public schools. The school systems that separated the races were to change this procedure with "all deliberate speed."

In 1957, in President Eisenhower's administration, a Civil Rights Act was passed. It was the first law regarding civil rights that had been passed in eighty-seven years. The main achievement was to give the Attorney General more power to see that Negroes were not denied the right to vote. Another act passed in

1960 extended this power.

The Negroes soon adopted other methods for winning further rights than laws passed by Congress. In Montgomery, Alabama, Negroes boycotted the buses until they stopped seating discrimination. "Sit-ins" at lunch counters won them the right to be served on equal terms in eating places. There were "kneel-ins" and "pray-ins" and "freedom rides" to win equal access to the rights belonging to all citizens. But for the most part, the methods used were non-violent.

Kennedy had been in sympathy with the movement and had worked for civil rights since he became a Senator in 1952. At the Democratic convention in 1960, he insisted on a strong civil rights statement in the platform. His telephone call to Mrs. Martin Luther King during the campaign had done much to win him the support of the Negroes. In the election, he won more than 75 percent of their votes. He realized that without this support, he might not have won.

Because of the Negro support of Kennedy, Dr. Martin Luther King urged, soon after the inauguration, that the President send a strong civil rights bill to Congress. Kennedy knew, however, that with his limited support in Congress there was no chance of getting such a bill passed. In addition, he would lose southern support for other bills that he thought were

without experience. Many of the Negroes were obliged to live in the slum areas of the city. For this housing they were charged extremely high rents and given little or no service.

In spite of the sympathy and efforts of President Kennedy, little real progress had been made on any of these points by 1963. In the South, fewer than 13,000 Negro children were attending schools with white children, and the segregation of schools in the North had actually increased. The right to vote was still hampered by various devices. The unemployment rate for the Negro was two and a half times as large as that for white workers.

In the spring of 1963, the civil rights movement began to turn public opinion in favor of the Negro. In April, a non-violent Negro protest march in Birmingham, Alabama, was broken up by the use of police dogs and other forms of police force. The sight of this in newspaper pictures and on television aroused national sympathy for the Negroes.

In May, another spectacle came when Governor Wallace of Alabama personally tried to stop the enrollment of two Negro students at the University of Alabama in Tuscaloosa. Earlier, in October, 1962, James Meredith, a Negro, had tried to enroll at the University of Mississippi in Oxford, Mississippi. A riot had followed and the President had been obliged to send in the National Guard to end the rioting. For the rest of Meredith's stay at the university he had been protected by United States marshals. Now, this time in Alabama, the President again had to order the National Guard to see that the students were enrolled.

That same evening, the President spoke to the nation on television regarding civil rights. In strong language he told of the living conditions of the Negroes. To change that situation was a "moral issue . . . as old as the Scriptures . . . and as clear as the Constitution," he said. He planned to send a bill to Congress the next week to show that "race has no place in American life or law."

On June 19, the President sent his bill to Congress. He realized that the stand he was now taking might have serious political results for him. A recent poll showed that four and a half million people who had voted for him in 1960 had now turned against him. "A good many programs I care about may go down the drain," he told the Negro leaders, "so we are putting a lot on the line."

The bill was discussed in Congress during the summer, but little action was taken. A march on Washington to influence Congress was planned for the summer by the civil rights leaders. On August 28, 1963, a quarter of a million people, both black and white, came to Washington for the march. Weeks of planning by the civil rights leaders and the Washington officials made the gathering take place without incident.

In the afternoon, the marchers gathered at the Lincoln Memorial. Political leaders were on the platform. The President had met the leaders in his office at the White House. Martin Luther King was the last one to speak. He told of his "dream" of Negro equality. The crowd shouted their approval, and were stirred to work toward making equality real. Then chanting their song, "We Shall Overcome," the vast crowd quietly left.

The march did little to induce Congress to pass the bill. In October, a compromise bill was worked out, but it was not passed until January, 1964.

Before the march to Washington, on June 23, 1963, President Kennedy had gone to Germany. He went first to Frankfurt and then to West Berlin. Three-fifths of the population were on the streets to cheer his motorcade. From the City Hall, he was taken to see the Berlin Wall. His face showed how shocked and angry he was at the sight.

Later the President spoke to a tremendous crowd in an open square. For the people who did not understand the issue between the free world and Communism, "Let them come to Berlin!" he cried, in English and then in German. The crowd roared its delight. "All free men are citizens of Berlin," he cried. "*Ich bin ein Berliner!*"

The wild response of the crowd to his words somewhat disturbed the President. Later he said, "If I had said, 'March to the Wall! Tear it down!' I believe they would have done it."

From Germany, the President went to Ireland. Here his journey was partly sentimental. He visited Dublin, and then went to New Ross in County Wexford from where his great-grandfather had come in 1849. There, as well as in Cork and Limerick, and when he spoke before the Irish Parliament, he was given a tremendous ovation. "This is not the land of my birth,"

President Kennedy views Berlin Wall, June, 1963.

Kennedy told the Irish, "but it is the land for which I hold the greatest affection."

From Ireland, Kennedy went to England to meet with Macmillan, and then to Italy. Pope John XXIII had died on June 1, and a new pope, Paul VI, had succeeded on June 21. He was an old friend of the Kennedy family.

Everywhere in Italy great crowds turned out to cheer John Kennedy. He left behind him in Europe the image of a young and idealistic, but tough-minded and determined executive. "In the summer of 1963," said one of his close aides and biographers, "John F. Kennedy could have been elected in every country in Europe."

On the other side of the globe was one of the most troublesome problems the world had to face—Vietnam. The situation in Vietnam grew steadily worse during Kennedy's administration.

In 1954, after the French granted independence to Vietnam, it was divided into North and South Vietnam. At that time, President Eisenhower had promised Ngo Dinh Diem, the Prime Minister of South Vietnam, support of his rule by the United States on condition that needed social reforms would be made. Diem, who had been in exile in the United States, was thought to be an honest and able man.

Diem, instead, became a despot. All power was in the hands of him and his family. In addition, Diem was openly disdainful of American democracy. However, he seemed a good administrator who would clean up the corruption in Saigon. In time, as no social reforms were made in South Vietnam, many people in the United States felt we were "over-committed."

Resentment against Diem grew in South Vietnam. In March, 1960, a rebellion was started by the National Liberation Party, or Viet Cong, as they were called. They were helped by the Communists in North Vietnam under their President, Ho Chi Minh. He gave them training, advice, and equipment, but the

President Kennedy confers with South Vietnam's Nguyyen Dinh Thuan.

rebels were mostly from South Vietnam. Guerrilla warfare was carried on, with attacks from ambush by the Viet Cong, and murder and torture of those who resisted. By the end of 1960, the Viet Cong had overrun half of the country. This was the situation when Kennedy became President.

In October, 1961, Kennedy sent advisers to investigate conditions in South Vietnam. They reported that the Vietnamese could put down the Viet Cong rebellion if they were given American aid.

Kennedy did not wish to make a military commitment. "The war can be won only if the Vietnamese realize it is their war," he said in a press conference. However, in December, Kennedy ordered an increase of U.S. troops in South Vietnam.

In 1962, our policy was to support the rule of Diem. Kennedy and his advisers thought we had "turned the corner in the war," and that it would be won "within the year." President Kennedy might not have thought so if he had given more thought to Vietnam. At the time he was more occupied with the test ban treaty and the civil rights struggle.

Newspapermen from the United States who were in Vietnam did not agree with these conclusions. They thought Diem was an Oriental despot. They felt the reports from our Embassy in South Vietnam were not truthful. In spite of the reassuring statements, they believed that the Viet Cong were as strong as ever, and that the government in Saigon showed no improvement. In addition, the South Vietnamese had no real motive for fighting. Under Diem, their life would not be improved very much if they won the war.

Kennedy's aim for Vietnam was to create a stable situation in which the people could choose their own government. The country had been at war for twenty years. He believed that if we withdrew our support from South Vietnam all the countries of Southeast Asia would be weakened. He thought that they would lose confidence in the democratic form of government and would turn to Communist countries for help. The control of the Communists could then be expanded all over Asia, even to include India. "So we are going to stay there," Kennedy said at a press conference.

Up to this time, Buddhists in Vietnam had not been persecuted, although they had few legal rights. In May, 1963, a group of Buddhists gathered to protest an order of Diem forbidding them to celebrate the birthday of Buddha. Diem's troops fired into the crowd, leaving many of them dead and wounded. Many Buddhists covered themselves with gasoline and burned themselves to death to protest this act. Now many young Vietnamese army officers as well as American newspapermen sympathized with the Buddhists and opposed Diem.

Then in August, Diem's troops attacked the Buddhist pagodas and arrested hundreds of Buddhists. People in the United States were shocked and surprised by the attacks, but our government still supported Diem. But now, in a press conference, Kennedy said that he thought the attacks on the Buddhists were unwise and that there should be "changes in policy and perhaps with personnel." This seemed to indicate that we would withdraw support from Diem.

Then in November, 1963, the generals in the Vietnamese army revolted. They seized government buildings and the broadcasting stations. Diem and his brother were killed. The whole affair was carried out by military leaders who thought Diem would turn the country into a police state.

President Kennedy now thought that his whole Vietnam policy needed to be thought out again. He felt that he had never given the problem sufficient attention. Our troops had grown from 2,000 to 16,000, and we had made no real gain. He hoped that with the overthrow of Diem more progress would be made. However, he realized that the fighting might go on for many years, because the Viet Cong would have no trouble getting recruits for their side.

10

PRESIDENT KENNEDY WAS LOOKING forward to the Presidential election of 1964. There was no question that he would be nominated again by the Democrats. All of the polls indicated that he would win with ease. He felt confident that if he won by a large majority, his bills for Medicare, federal aid to education, tax reduction, and civil rights would be passed in the next session of Congress.

He thought that Senator Barry Goldwater would be the Republican candidate for President. If so, there would be a real issue in the election with a Democratic liberal against a Republican conservative.

At times, Kennedy looked even beyond 1964 to what he would do when his second term was over. Perhaps he would return to Congress like John Quincy Adams. Or he would publish a newspaper, or travel, or write a book. In one way or another, he would still continue in public service.

The years in office had made some difference in John Kennedy. He was older looking now. There were lines in his face and gray hair in the thick mop of red-brown hair. He still moved quickly and with easy grace, and was confident in his bearing and manner. His wit and humor had not diminished, especially when he was in private or with close associates.

Caroline, John, Jr., and President Kennedy welcoming Mrs. Kennedy home from a European vacation, 1963.

The summer of 1963 held sadness for the Kennedys. In August, the Kennedys had a third child, christened Patrick Bouvier. The baby was born in Newport with a breathing difficulty. The child lived only thirty-nine hours, in spite of every effort of the doctors at a Boston hospital. The young parents grieved as any mother and father would. But the job of being President leaves little time for personal sorrow.

On Thursday, November 21, President Kennedy left Washington for a tour of Texas. Mrs. Kennedy went with him. One city on the tour was Dallas. Most of the people there, especially the business leaders, were Protestant and strongly conservative. Many were bitterly against Kennedy, not only because of his political views but because of his religion.

A month before the President was to go to Texas, Adlai Stevenson had gone to Dallas. During his speech, he had been heckled. When he had come out of the hall, a crowd of pickets had pushed against him. A woman had hit him on the head with a sign, and a man had spat in Stevenson's face.

Because of these incidents, those preparing for the President's visit to Dallas were concerned about his safety, or at least, the respect with which he would be treated. On the other hand, if Dallas were not included in the tour, there would be criticism.

All went well in Texas as the tour began. Cheering crowds turned out to greet the party in San Antonio, Houston, and Fort Worth. On Friday, November 22, the President was to go from Fort Worth to Dallas for a motorcade and luncheon.

In the morning of November 22, Kennedy read *The Dallas Morning News*. It contained a full-page advertisement headed, "WELCOME MR. KENNEDY TO DALLAS," claiming to speak for the "American-thinking citizens" of Dallas. The heading was followed by a list of insulting questions, all indicating that the President was at least a Communist if not a traitor. "How can people write such things?" Kennedy asked in disgust.

From Fort Worth, the party went by plane to Dallas. Shortly before noon, the motorcade began. It was a beautiful day: "Kennedy weather," it was said. Cheering crowds lined the streets and increased in number as the parade neared the center of the town. Only a few anti-Kennedy signs were seen.

The President rode in the first car with Mrs. Kennedy, who looked radiant in a bright pink suit and hat to match. Texas Governor Connally and his wife were on the jump seats. Secret Service men protecting the President rode in his car and the next. The bubble top of the President's car had been removed, and the bullet-proof windows were open. He stood up most of the time waving to the crowd. As the motorcade slowed to make a turn, Kennedy sat down and began to chat with the Connallys.

"You can't say that Dallas is not friendly to you today," said Mrs. Connally.

There was a sharp crackling sound. The President jerked sharply and clutched his neck. Governor Connally turned around. The sound could have been a motorcycle backfiring, but as the sound was repeated, there was no mistaking it. Someone was shooting at the President's car. Later there were conflicting reports of how many shots were fired and where they came from.

As the Governor turned, he tumbled into the arms of his wife. The President fell forward into the arms of Mrs. Kennedy, and there was a burst of blood in the back of his head. It had all happened in about six seconds.

"Oh, my God!" cried Mrs. Kennedy. "They have shot my husband! Jack ! Jack!"

When the limousine pulled up at the Parkland Hospital, the President lay unconscious on his back, his head cradled in his wife's lap. In minutes, both the President and Governor Connally were being carried on stretchers into emergency rooms.

President and Mrs. Kennedy and Governor Connally, Dallas, Nov. 22, 1963.

Doctors worked desperately to save the President's life, but there was no hope. Mrs. Kennedy stood quietly in the room as they worked, but her eyes were filled with fear. In a short time, two priests arrived. One administered the last rites of the Catholic Church. In the meantime, Governor Connally was also being examined. His wounds were serious, but not fatal.

At 1:33 P.M., a press aide, red-eyed and with shaking voice, told the waiting reporters, "President John F. Kennedy died at approximately 1:00 P.M. central standard time here in Dallas. He died of a gunshot wound in the brain."

There was a stunned hush for a moment after the statement was read. Then the reporters rushed to the telephones. All over the country, people listening or watching as the news was broadcast had that same stunned, unbelieving reaction.

That afternoon, Dallas police arrested a man named Lee Harvey Oswald who was suspected of being the assassin. Oswald was never brought to trial, however, for two days later, he was himself killed. As he was being transferred from the city jail to the county jail, a Dallas man named Jack Ruby sprang from a crowd of newspapermen and shot Oswald. The full circumstances of the assassination may never be known. Ruby died in prison three years after the event, still bitter and confused.

After Johnson became President, he appointed a commission headed by Supreme Court Chief Justice Earl Warren to investigate John Kennedy's death. The Warren Commission concluded that Lee Harvey Oswald was the killer, and that he had acted alone and was not part of a conspiracy. But there were many controversial points on which they based their conclusions, and the report they made was disputed.

About three o'clock on the day President Kennedy died, the bronze casket containing his body was taken to Air Force One, the presidential plane. Mrs. Kennedy accompanied the casket.

About 3:30, the oath of office was administered to Lyndon B. Johnson by Judge Sarah T. Hughes, an old friend of the Johnsons. The brief ceremony was over by 3:38. "Let's get airborne" was the first order of the new President.

The plane arrived in Washington about six o'clock. Waiting in the dusk were high officials of the government, foreign diplomats, and many others whose grief brought them there. Robert Kennedy and Ted Sorenson, both white-faced and grief-stricken, stood near the front. The door of the plane opened. For a moment, those who waited almost expected to see a tall, slim man give them his familiar wave and grin. But there was only a gleam of light on a bronze coffin.

The new President and his wife stepped forward to the waiting microphones. "This is a sad time for all people," he began his brief statement. "I will do my best. That is all that I can do. I ask for your help and God's."

While Mrs. Kennedy was on the plane coming to Washington, and during the hours of the night, in spite of her shock and grief, she had made plans for her husband's funeral. By its dignity and beauty, she hoped somehow to erase the memory of the terrible crime that had ended his life so cruelly. She could plan for the funeral because she had a deep sense of history, and she knew what her husband would have liked. She requested that the same procedures be followed as with the death of President Lincoln.

Although she was exhausted when she came to the White House, Mrs. Kennedy stayed to see that the details were carried out. The bronze coffin was placed on a high black catafalque in the East Room. The tall windows and great chandeliers were draped in black, and the small lights had been dimmed. This was as it had been when President Lincoln lay in state.

In the morning, the Kennedy family attended a private Mass in the East Room and then retired for the day. Hundreds of messages of sympathy were pouring into the White House now. All over the world, flags were flying at half-mast, and people were expressing their shock and grief.

In Berlin and in Bern, Switzerland, weeping throngs marched through the streets at night carrying flaming torches. Requiem Masses were being said everywhere. In all of the great cities, people watched or listened to broadcasts and wept and prayed. Long lines of people came to the American Embassies in every foreign capital to sign memorial books and state their sentiments.

Khrushchev called at the American Embassy in Moscow to sign the book. His face showed his sombre thoughts. Later Khrushchev said that President Kennedy had been a man with whom he could talk. He would miss the close relationship that was beginning between them. Mrs. Khrushchev did nothing to hide her tears as she added her signature.

Early Saturday morning, President Johnson met with leaders in Congress and the administration, and with former Presidents Truman and Eisenhower, who had quickly come to Washington. One of the first acts of President Johnson was to proclaim that Monday would be a day of national mourning.

The world was to see the orderly process by which one President in the United States succeeded another, even in a time of sudden change. Johnson was the Vice-President best prepared to succeed of any the U.S. had ever had. He had sat with the President at every time an important decision was made. He had been briefed on every situation in the administration.

There was a cold rain nearly all day on Saturday. Beginning at eleven o'clock, the government leaders in the United States and then the diplomats from other countries came to the White House to pay their respects to the dead President.

About one o'clock on Sunday, the bronze coffin was taken to the Capitol. Mrs. Kennedy, dressed now in black and holding the hands of her two children, stood on the portico. The children now knew what had happened.

The young pallbearers, representing the armed services, placed the coffin on a caisson drawn by six gray-white horses. Riders were on three of the horses. The other three were saddled but riderless. A fourth man rode along the side.

Behind the caisson, a soldier led a spirited, riderless black horse. A pair of boots turned backward and a sword in a scabbard hung from the saddle. They were the symbols of a warrior who has fallen.

The streets were thronged with silent people, many of them weeping, as the procession moved slowly along to the beat of muffled drums. Up the long steps of the Capitol, the bearers carried their burden. Mrs. Kennedy and her children and Robert Kennedy were the first to follow. After them came the rest of the family and the government officials.

The coffin was placed on a catafalque in the Rotunda of the Capitol. It was the same catafalque that had been used when President Lincoln lay in state. There were eulogies now from the government leaders. Mrs. Kennedy's eyes were blurred with tears, but she stood erect as the tributes were paid, and so did Caroline. She was not yet six years old, but she realized her great loss.

Little John Kennedy grew restless during the speeches, and someone took him to the office of the

Mrs. John F. Kennedy, Caroline, John Jr., and Robert Kennedy follow the casket of the slain President up the steps of the Capitol Building.

Speaker of the House. He was given a small flag to hold. "I want one for my daddy," said John, not yet understanding, and so he was given another flag.

When the tributes were over, Mrs. Kennedy and Caroline knelt for a brief time beside the coffin. The young widow kissed the flag. Caroline raised the flag a little and gave the coffin a gentle pat. The ceremony in the Capitol was ended.

151

All Sunday afternoon in Washington after President Kennedy's body had been brought to the Capitol, and until nine o'clock on Monday morning, long lines of people slowly moved into the Rotunda. The line was two miles long, and it took some people six hours before they entered the Capitol. In all, about 250,000 people passed the coffin and the motionless guards. There was still a large crowd waiting to enter when, reluctantly, the great doors were closed.

It was clear and cold on Monday morning. By this time, the heads of state from all over the world had come to Washington to attend the funeral of President Kennedy. At the gates of the White House were those who would march to St. Matthew's Cathedral, about a mile away. Mrs. Kennedy had broken all precedents by stating that she would march in the procession. President and Mrs. Johnson stated that they would do the same in spite of the protests of the Secret Service men.

In the first line of the march was Mrs. Kennedy between her husband's two brothers. She held her head high and walked with straight, long strides, though her long widow's veil hid her tear-filled eyes. Behind her walked the rest of the President's family, and then President Johnson and his family. Leaders of the government mingled with the great men of other countries. President de Gaulle of France, Emperor Haile

Selassie of Ethiopia, King Baudouin of Belgium, Queen Fredericka of Greece, Prince Philip of England, and Chancellor Erhard of West Germany were near the head of the line. There were more than two hundred in all, with Secret Service men everywhere in an effort to protect this most distinguished assemblage. Never had so many high personages been together at one time.

The bells tolled from St. John's Episcopal Church across from the White House. The bands played funeral marches. The bagpipes of the Black Watch sounded shrilly in between. Mrs. Kennedy had remembered her husband's pleasure when the Black Watch band had played on the White House lawn on Veterans' Day, scarcely two weeks before. She had asked that they be included in the funeral procession. With it all was the sound of drums beating in slow rhythm. A million silent people lined the streets, and many of them wept and prayed.

At St. Matthew's Cathedral, Caroline and John Jr. joined their mother. Cardinal Cushing, who had married the Kennedys and christened and buried their children, was waiting at the entrance to receive the family and express his sympathy.

The funeral service was simple and brief. Cardinal Cushing said a low Mass. "May the angels, dear Jack, lead you into Paradise," he said at the end of his prayers. There was no eulogy. Instead, portions from John Kennedy's speeches were read.

Then the coffin was carried out of the church. Mrs. Kennedy waited at the entrance with her children. Caroline stood with tear-filled eyes and tightened lips. Little John looked around, alert and curious as he watched the strange pageantry. This was his third birthday, but he probably did not know about the gay presents and birthday cake he had missed. Mrs. Kennedy leaned down and whispered to him. Then as the casket passed, the little boy's hand went up in salute. It was a gesture that would be long remembered.

The burial was to be in the Arlington National Cemetery, where all who have served with honor in the armed services of the United States have the right to be buried. Arlington had been selected by Mrs. Kennedy, rather than Boston. "He belongs to the people," she had said.

Slowly the funeral procession moved past the Lincoln Memorial and then across the Arlington Memorial Bridge. The throbbing drums slowly and regularly repeated their muffled notes.

The burial service was brief but moving. The National Anthem was played. There was an overflight of fifty planes, one for each state. Then Air Force One,

President Kennedy's funeral cortege on the way to Arlington Cemetery. The riderless horse (extreme right) follows the coffin.

the President's plane, flew over alone. A drill team of Irish soldiers went through their paces. President Kennedy had seen this ceremony when he had visited Ireland. Mrs. Kennedy remembered his pleasure in the sight. She had asked that the team be flown to Washington for the funeral.

The presidential salute of twenty-one guns thundered and echoed from the hills. Cardinal Cushing said a prayer. Taps were sounded. The flag that had covered the casket was folded and handed to Mrs. Kennedy. Then she moved forward and lit the torch that is to burn forever on President Kennedy's grave. It was "something living," she had said. After her, the President's brothers each put a light to the flame. Then hand in hand, Mrs. Kennedy and Robert silently followed all those who had watched the beautiful ceremony.

There was just one more duty for Mrs. Kennedy to assume before that day was over. She felt she must receive and thank all the dignitaries who had come from foreign lands to the funeral. "It would be most ungracious for me not to have all those people in our house," she had said. So with the brothers of the President to assist her, with gentle smile and composed air, she greeted each representative in the East Room and the Red Room, and thanked them for the homage they had paid her husband.

Will John F. Kennedy go down in history as a great President? That is hard to determine. There was so much he had planned and set in motion, and, by his own estimate, so little had been accomplished.

The Presidency of John F. Kennedy was a time of change. The great crises of the past thirty years were over—the Depression, the Second World War, and the beginning of atomic power. Only the fearful threat of how that power might be used hung over the nation. This was the time to look forward to the future.

President Kennedy was a symbol of that change. In his inaugural he had said, "The torch has been passed to a new generation of Americans." President Kennedy belonged to that "new generation." He was the first of our presidents to be born in the twentieth century. His youth, his energy, his modern outlook, and his ability to grow put him in that era. He was a man of ideas, but also a man of action. "He was an idealist without illusions," said his wife who knew him best of all.

The history of the future may put President Kennedy in the first rank not so much because of what he achieved, but because of his fight for what was the best for mankind, and his deep desire to have reason rather than force bring peace to the world. The goals he set out to achieve, and the standards of excellence he tried to establish, will live for many years to come. He changed the spirit of America.

BIBLIOGRAPHY

AMORY, CLEVELAND, *The Proper Bostonians*. New York, E. P. Dutton & Co., Inc., 1947.

BURNS, JAMES MACGREGOR, *John Kennedy, A Political Profile*. New York, Harcourt, Brace & World, Inc., 1959.

Four Days: *The Historical Record of the Death of President Kennedy*. New York, United Press International and American Heritage, 1964.

LINCOLN, EVELYN, *My Twelve Years With John Kennedy*. New York, David McKay & Co., Inc., 1965.

SALINGER, PIERRE, *With Kennedy*. Garden City, N. Y. Doubleday & Company, Inc., 1966.

SCHLESINGER, ARTHUR M., JR., *A Thousand Days*. Boston, Houghton Mifflin Company, 1965.

SCHOOR, GENE, *Young John Kennedy*. New York, MacFadden-Bartell Corp., 1965.

SIDEY, HUGH, *John F. Kennedy, President*. New York, Atheneum Publishers, 1963.

SORENSON, THEODORE, *Kennedy*. New York, Harper & Row, Publishers, 1965.

WHALEN, RICHARD J., *The Founding Father*. New York, The New American Library, 1964.

WHITE, THEODORE, *The Making of the President, 1960*. New York, Atheneum Publishers, 1961.

———, *The Making of the President, 1964*. New York, Atheneum Publishers, 1965.

INDEX